I found this book not only beautifully written and eloquent, but heartfelt and inspiring. I had to stop several times to process what Cyndi had written and think about my own life and how her message pertains to it. I felt Bre in this book. Bre was the person that I (and many others) would go to for inspiration and a fresh perspective. She often had a book for me to read that would be helpful. I kept thinking THIS would be a book she would have given me. Cyndi wrote, "My daughter, Bre, had an open and very curious mind. She would ask questions, lots of questions." The author did this here, and answered what she found to be true; and has covered the questions that rose up in me while I was reading. I have felt a sense of hypocrisy toward organized religion, but this book helped me separate those feelings from God. It makes so much sense to me. I, also, resonated with what was written about choices and the feelings attached to them. I feel uplifted and hopeful after reading this book.

— Joanna Ford

If you have been searching for answers, or have been skeptical of God's existence, you may find the answers here. Cyndi's search applies logic with science and spirituality to uncover the mystery behind the questions many of us ask. The loss of our beloved Breana created a need in Cyndi to find facts, and she shares them with us in *When You Think About It*. This book gives validation to the many ideas and thoughts I have had over the years. I found her book easy to read and thought provoking at the same time.

—Deb Kocher

A thought provoking look at the hereafter, and our religious beliefs in relation to today's science. *When You Think About It,* opens that door.

— Ruthie and Chuck Lee

After reading this book it brought up a lot of old feelings and beliefs. Being one of the NDE's, I experienced a lot of the feelings of this author before and after the experience. Before my NDE I was unsure of God and what it meant. It was too hard for me to fathom there was one being that created all of the universe. Going through my NDE was the best thing that could happen to me. I felt more love than you could imagine. Like I told Cyndi, *think of all the people you love and multiply it by ten* and you aren't even close to what your soul is feeling. I believe she hit the nail on the head with her depiction of soul energy. It is in all of us, we just have to listen to it and let it happen. LOVE is the answer.

— Stacy Grieb

When Cyndi began her journey years ago, I didn't realize I would be taking it with her. Yet, that is what happened. *When You Think About It* is the result of that journey and one I am happy to have been involved with. My faith, which was nonexistent, increased infinity times infinity during this time. I now believe that after my life is done here, I have a home to return to.

— Les Hanning

Wow! It looked like hours and hours of research went into the writing of *When You Think About It*. I thought it was great. It had me dripping on page 92, because Cyndi explained who Breana was so clearly. Great job!

— Arlene Gallagher

When You Think About It, reads like a conversation. In fact, Bre and I had many conversations like it throughout our friendship that began when we were fifteen. Another day, I would love to tell her mom who she was to me, and how amazing it is that she brought up this glowing spirit that had the maturity in high school to philosophize religion with an open mind.

— Sarah Kummer

From the beginning the author shows compassion, as well as, confusion for the loss of her daughter, Bre. Compassion because she wants her daughter back and confusion because she has no idea where she is and cannot accept the "normal" answers of death. Where did she go and why did she have to go? Will she ever see her again? This book is the journey the author took to find answers, and in the travels of her mind found much more than that. We loved this book!

— Gene and Wendy Goosman

When You Think About It

When You Think About It

A Fact-finding Journey to Discover My Daughter's Eternal Home, and the Knowledge I Wish I Had While Raising Her

by

Cynthia M. Mitchell

When You Think About It

Copyright © 2015 by Cynthia M. Mitchell

978-1-78324-014-2 (paperback)
978-1-78324-015-9 (dustjacket)
978-1-78324-016-6 (eBook)

Whilst every effort has been made to ensure that the information contained within this book is correct at the time of going to press, the author and publisher can take no responsibility for the errors or omissions contained within.

Edited by Jo-Ann Langseth
Published and designed by Wordzworth Publishing

Disclaimer

This book is the result of every thought I had about all the books I've read throughout my life and in these last few years. If you think you see yourself in this book, rest assured there were other authors with similar thoughts. It was those interlinking thoughts that caused me to form my own thoughts and put them together into one book.

Contents

Each chapter stands alone and represents a topic I explored in my journey to find answers. Each paragraph represents my thoughts about that topic. As in most research, no one book held all of the answers, so I read many and then incorporated what I had discovered into *When You Think About It*.

In memory of my awesome daughter, Breana

and

dedicated to her incredible son, Owen

Preface

At an early age you begin to ask yourself questions. Lots of questions. Some of these questions you can find answers to, but many you tell yourself have no answers, so you tuck them away for another day. That day came for me when I lost my only child, Breana. The pain was immense and the questions unending. Where is she? Will I see her again? Why isn't she here for her son? If everything has a purpose, what could the purpose of losing her possibly be? Is there really a God, and what or who is He? For me life had no reason without her in it. Is this physical world we live in the only reality? If so, what is the point?

I became obsessed with finding her and with answering those long-ago questions. When faith is not enough, where do you turn? The things we learn as children become the facts we base our decisions on. Are they true—or just accepted and passed down through time? I began reading intensely. I had an interest in anything written by mediums, psychics, doctors, nurses, scientists, near-death experiencers, and hospice workers; anyone who had something to say on the subject was where I looked.

I noticed that early physicists were being quoted in some of the books I was reading. Why? I wanted to learn more. What is this quantum world and how do we fit into it? I realized that greater minds than mine had written these books and I wasn't sure I could understand them. The concentration I needed was unavailable to me in the beginning.

Determination drove me forward however, and in time the concentration came.

I was surprised when I could see the lines cross between God (not religion) and science. I began to see God as the ultimate scientist and not a god at all. In fact, He is very different from the human god I had learned about as a child. There were many reasons to be afraid of that God.

I wondered why I had not come across a book that incorporated all of these subjects into one. Had no one else seen the correlation? Could I write something for my grandson that would help him understand what I understood so clearly? I began taking notes. Those notes became *When You Think About It.*

Foreword

Cyndi Mitchell has written about one of the most profound gifts a child could have ever given a parent, in her book called *When You Think About It*. However, this gift is also one of the most costly. It is difficult to imagine that the gut wrenching pain from the death of a loved one can bring forth a powerful gift. However, this juxtaposition is exactly what Cyndi captures with intimate honesty.

Many years ago, I found myself in one of the most difficult situations of my life. My friends car had slid on the ice into the river. I dove in again and again in an attempt to rescue them. Defeated in the frigid darkness of those swirling waters, I returned to shore exhausted and fighting off hypothermia.

I spent years struggling with the loss, as well as the ceaseless internal questioning of what if… What if I had done this or what if I had done that? The internal questioning was a perpetual torture that I knew I had to stop if I wanted to remain healthy.

The passing away of these two friends introduced a challenging journey of grief. From this journey, I made a discovery. There was a gift that was left behind by my two friends. As a result, this gift became an integral part of the book I wrote, "Death of an Ordinary Life." Needless to say, my life had been changed forever.

Today, I am a mental health counselor and I have had the honor of joining others as they travel through their arduous journey of grief. I discovered that when we follow our grief, there is always a beautiful gift that is left behind.

I have known Cyndi Mitchell all my life, and she is as honest, hard working, passionate, and motivated as they come. The loss of her daughter was nothing short of devastating. Bre was such an amazing person that inspired everyone she met. I know that it is cliché to speak highly of someone that has passed but Bre was actually, one of those people. I always found myself inspired to be more compassionate, considerate, and contemplative after being around her.

Cyndi invites us to take a very personal journey with her as she tried to sort through the loss of her daughter in, *When You Think About It*. Armed with the same fearless curiosity of her daughter, Cyndi discovers the wonderful gift that Bre left behind for her. Now Cyndi is sharing this wonderful gift with everyone.

When You Think About It is a wonderful story for anyone searching for those tough answers in life. Cyndi gives us a chance to contemplate life, death, spirit, religion, science, and grief in a very thoughtful and compassionate way.

—Aaron Mitchell, MS, LMHCA

Acknowledgments

I first want to thank my daughter for leading me down the path to discovery of where she truly is, and to the loving God she's at home with now. Secondly, thank you to my grandson Owen, who was the inspiration for me to write it down for him to have one day. They are and always will be the most important people in my life.

Thanks to Les for supporting me through years of deep sadness and listening to all my new discoveries. I'm sure he wanted to roll his eyes but he never did. In fact, he was very encouraging. It was through all that talk that I began to acquire deeper thoughts into the many mysteries we live with. I am forever grateful.

There are so many people I want to thank! Kay Maynard, thanks for getting me through work each day and also listening to my ideas. I am so lucky to have you as my friend. Invaluable too were my sister, Debbie Kocher; my mom, Doris Mitchell; my son-in-law, Ben Langan, who read the first very incomplete draft but still encouraged me to keep writing; and my dear friends Chuck and Ruthie Lee, who would never have read a book like this had I not written it, yet found it thought-provoking—which is the sole purpose of the book.

In the beginning, I became discouraged and overwhelmed with all the information and disorganized thoughts I was experiencing. When I expressed this to Madeline Cross, she volunteered to come to my home and sit with me in my little bedroom office. Together, we went over what I had started until I could see the light, encouraging me to continue on. Thank you for the love and support. You are awesome!

Thank you, Gene and Wendy Goosman, for being in my and Bre's life and for your encouraging words during this process. Thank you to Bre's friends, who became the beta readers for the completed manuscript and for the reviews. I can see why you were ALL her best friends, and I loved hearing the stories you still carry with you.

I want to acknowledge Beth Jusino, who offered a one-day seminar at the University of Washington into the confusing world of publishing, and to Karen Sloan for finding and attending that class with me.

Lastly, I want to thank my editor, Jo-Ann Langseth, for the beautiful job she did in making me sound more intelligent than I am. It has been an incredible journey!

CHAPTER ONE

My Life Unfolds

I began to see that religion creates
separation and fear. This could not be
God's intent. What are we missing?

When you think about it, aren't you one of the lucky ones to have been born to parents who loved and nurtured you? As a child, you assume all children are treated the same as you are. It's very sad to learn this isn't always true. As a hairdresser, I've had the opportunity to talk with people who have dealt with things children should never have to deal with.

The love or rejection you feel as a child has a huge impact on your interactions with people and life itself. I was one of the lucky ones to have been given the skills from loving parents to deal with and enjoy life, without having to overcome such horrific challenges.

My life began in 1948. I was preceded by two brothers and followed by a sister. My first brother died at birth. My mom struggled with that, since her religion taught her that without baptism, you couldn't make it to heaven. Can you imagine a God, who loves you unconditionally, not taking you into His arms because you didn't get sprinkled at the baptismal font on Earth? That just didn't compute. Mom came to realize that, too.

Dad, having a Mormon background, was certain you had until you were eight years old to be baptized. Jesus said, "Let the children come to me, and I will bless them." So the Mormons believe that children are to be blessed and by the age of eight, they are old enough to be baptized with the knowledge of why it's happening. They also believe you need to be completely submerged in water and not just sprinkled to be recognized by God, since that's the technique John the Baptist used. Obviously, we all joined the Mormon Church and went every Sunday. It was a great relief to know we're all saved – unless you're one of those who believe Mormons are pagan and are not saved after all.

You see, Mormons believe God, Jesus, and the Holy Spirit are three separate entities, while other Christian religions believe they are all one entity. This is known as the Trinity. Some religions believe the Bible is clear in saying that Jesus was God in human form; others believe they are Father and Son. It's a mystery to me. Why is it that people spend so much time interpreting the Bible, yet cannot reconcile this one issue? Is it because it's not an issue for God? Can it be He has more important things to concern Himself with? Sadly, man has taken something as beautiful as God's love for us (all of us) and used it to judge their fellow humans, even fight wars over. Why do we feel the need to be more righteous than the other? Religion is based on faith, not fact, so what makes your faith better than someone else's faith? I was beginning to lose faith in any religion.

My brother was a year older than I. It was great having an older brother, at least when I was older. Growing up, he could overpower me when Mom wasn't looking and get most anything he wanted. God forbid if anyone else ever tried, though! Yes, he was my protector, my buddy, and a very good source of help with any math problem I had in school.

What fun we had building cabins in the woods of the old farm we grew up on, sliding down the snowy hills, and fixing beautiful mud-and-berry dinners served on a bed of skunk cabbage that grew in the swamp on our property. I especially liked building roads and tunnels around the huge evergreen tree in our front yard with its exposed root system. When his buddies came over, my brother didn't like including me in the action. Mom usually stepped in (when I tattled on him) to convince them of how much fun I could be. Then there was the BB gun. He would shoot birds out of the cherry tree and I would give them each a funeral. It was very sad for me to see them die, but we did like those cherries they kept gobbling, and they somehow couldn't learn the concept of sharing. I doubt that my brother could do that today, but that was then and this is now.

Eight years later our sister was born. She was so tiny, we could dress her in my doll clothes. Needless to say, we were very proud of our new baby sister. Mom would let us rock her in the big rocking chair. She seemed to love that and so did we. Little did we know she would grow to be a bit of a pest. She liked being with us, and our little reporter made sure there were no longer any secrets from Mom and Dad. Even when you spelled it, she would repeat the spelling to them. We did have a way of keeping her contained, however. We had some old tires Dad let us play with and soon discovered she couldn't get out when we put her in the middle. What bullies older brothers and sisters can be! Although, in our defense, when it came to eating her peas, we would eat them for her as soon as Mom and Dad left the table to watch the evening news.

My dad had a guitar he would pull out from time to time. We loved hearing him sing cowboy songs and yodel. I think that's why I go soft when I hear someone play guitar and sing, and is why I have a guitar at my cabin for anyone willing to play it. My dad stopped playing that old guitar years ago and I don't know what became of it. How fun it would have been to keep it! In fact, there are a lot of things I might have kept and a lot of things I would ask my dad, if I still could. Like what he thought when he met Mom or held his first baby. Who were his best friends growing up? What was his favorite color, his favorite book, his proudest moment, his favorite car? So many questions left unanswered. When a person is with you, you don't ordinarily see the significance of those questions. After they're gone, you realize all you have are the memories, and you wish there were many more of them.

The advice you get from your parents is invaluable, but you don't always realize it at the moment it is given. Something I remember my mom telling me was, "Always be able to take care of yourself; have some sort of career path." - I chose hairdressing. It seemed to be a fun thing to do. Although I worked at Boeing for a couple years before actually going to school, it proved to be a very important decision.

I was married in 1970 and divorced six years later. Our baby, Breana, was six months old at the time. Afraid and alone, I knew I had to take care of myself and my daughter. Divorce was such a dirty word in the 1970s. I first had to get over that and accept my true identity as a single mom and move through it. My baby was my highest priority. With the support of family to help watch her, I was able to extend my hours at the salon. I was always worried about having enough money – and what if she wanted to go to college? Would I be able to make that happen? And what about maintaining the yard and house? All of those things seemed so very important to me.

I knew that to secure the future, I would need to own my own salon. Aware of the commitment involved, it was actually something I never really wanted to do. But seeing no other option, I began planning for just that. My first step toward that goal was to form a partnership with the man I worked for. That worked well for a few years, until he and his wife went through a divorce of their own, putting me in the middle of a not-so-friendly battle. I loved both of them and wouldn't pick a side. We had two salons at the time. I offered to buy the one I was working in and just like that, I was on my own. His wife, who was once my partner, was now a hairdresser working for me. She also became my landlord after the divorce settlement left the building to her.

She was now a single mom with two children of her own, and the same concerns I had as a single mom. The building was not in the best location for a salon. We knew we would have to move one day, when she felt more solid in her new circumstances. There is no retirement in this business, so how you invest your money is important. Real estate, I believed, was the best place to put it. Knowing that, I began looking for a location to purchase and relocate the salon.

It took three years for that time to come around. Of course, I had to obtain a loan to purchase the building, so off to the banks I went. Armed with a surveyed list of clients saying they would follow us to the new location, and a projection done by my accountant (a study of probable growth), the banks trusted me enough to take the risk. Plus, it helped that I owned my own home. Collateral is always a good thing. I had my mom and dad to thank for that, since my ex-husband and I had purchased it from them years earlier at a very good price.

The building I found needed extensive work, basically to be gutted and fitted with all new everything. That was quite a learning experience in itself. My daughter, Bre, was twelve by this time and wasn't too sure anyone would come to us, judging from the way it looked. Its green paint was chipping and moss covered the roof. I certainly had to agree with her on that one.

I hired a contractor, who was a client of the salon, to help put the building together. The building of course needed new wiring, plumbing, and pretty much everything imaginable. The contractor, Gene Goosman, took the plans a salon designer had drawn for me and made them work. They certainly wouldn't have worked the way they were drawn. Needless to say, Bre and I became good friends with him and his family during this time.

It was also during this time that I met my second husband. The perfect man. Oh my, how blind love can be! That marriage lasted three very long years, as I found myself supporting him and his various business ventures. That pretty much took up most of my energy. Trying to work on a doomed marriage, when I could have been spending it with my daughter in her high school years. We don't realize how much our children hurt when we hurt. If only we could relive some parts of our lives with the knowledge gained from those mistakes – without having to make them in the first place. What a fantasy!

During this time, Bre and I spent a lot of weekends with Gene and Wendy Goosman at their cabin on Mt. Baker, skiing and just being with them. They will probably never know what a comfort it was to be with such a healthy and loving family. Something I knew I would never be able to give my daughter. Their son and Bre became best friends and she referred to Wendy as her second mom.

In conversation one day, the idea came up that we should buy our own cabin. Of course, this was Bre's idea. I was opposed; too much responsibility. I had a house and a salon to maintain. How could I take on anything else? She had the solution: she would take care of the cabin and had saved enough for the down payment. That made it a little hard to say no.

Now, some might wonder how a young person could have saved that much money. I was always very careful with money, but she took it to a new level. When she was very young, I gave her an old checkbook. In it she would track the money she earned from allowance and any gift she received. Then, when she wanted something, we would look in her checkbook to see if there was enough money. She would then write me a check and deduct it from her check register. As she got older and had a job in an espresso bar, she took it to a new level again, putting the money in categories. A percentage went into a house fund, a car fund, and entertainment. She never bought things she didn't need, and wouldn't dream of charging anything. She loved things that had already been used. She just couldn't see spending money on something new, when secondhand would do. Education was my responsibility. She wasn't too interested in college, but I convinced her to take a few classes. She said it was just to humor me. She was a good sport that way.

Well, we bought that cabin in the woods. It was an amazing place, where worries seemed to melt away. She told me I was a different person at the cabin, and that was why. I didn't feel the stress of the business or anything else, only the joy of hanging out with my daughter. We spent holidays there and enjoyed great meals around the picnic table, which became our dining table. We upholstered cushions on the benches with our trusty staple gun and they were transformed. We strung popcorn and made our own Christmas decorations, which I will always keep. We became so confident with that staple gun that we upholstered the old furniture that was left there. I must say, I wasn't as confident about that as Bre was, but she was right – it turned out great. It's amazing what you can do with very little money.

When New Year's Eve rolled around, Bre and some of her friends decided they would celebrate up there. I warned her it could snow and it did. They were snowed in and lost power. With nothing to do, they decided it would be fun to jump off the second-story deck to the snow below. She couldn't resist telling me about it, even knowing I wasn't going to see the same humor in it that they did.

Bre was always telling on herself. I once told her, when she was very young, that her eyes would turn green if she ever lied to me. If she told me the truth, she wouldn't get in trouble, but if she lied, she would. I guess she believed me, because we didn't have too many secrets. Anyway, we had many great talks and wonderful walks in the fresh air and memories I will cherish forever.

It wasn't long after that I met my best friend, Les. He seemed to like the cabin as much as we did. Bre and I had done some remodeling, like moving cupboards around, but Les helped take it to the next level. Together we were able to finish the basement. We completed the half-plumbed bathroom and added cedar to the cement walls and ceiling. Together we transformed that ugly basement into a very cozy place where our friends could stay. He seemed to really enjoy any project we could dream up, but mostly I noticed how much he enjoyed my daughter. That spoke volumes to me.

Now might be a good time to go into relationships. As I said earlier, I was married twice. That was one time too many – more than I thought would ever happen to me. After all, didn't our vows say "Till death us do part"? I actually believed that, and the church had instilled it in me. It was a covenant you made with God. Needless to say, I don't have the same beliefs anymore, and even some churches have become more tolerant in interpreting that mandate.

So when Bre asked me, "Mom, do you think Ben and I should get married?" my answer reflected my experience. "If you think you have the ingredients to bake the cake, then bake the cake. But, if you find an ingredient is missing after you put it into the oven to bake, then I believe in divorce." She, however, didn't share that view and I was actually glad she didn't. It also told me she was sure she had found the right man and had already put a lot of thought into it. It's a serious decision and shouldn't be taken lightly. I just wanted to make sure she'd never feel like a failed marriage meant she was a failure. That was the point I wanted to make. Seeming "failures" are simply experiences that you learn from, which I believe is the reason we're here in the first place. Ideally, you learn it the first time and don't have to learn the same lesson over and over.

When you're sad, your children are sad, too. As much as you think you're protecting them, they go through each heartache with you. Bre never met anyone I dated unless I had been out with him three times. That was my little rule. I thought it would be too confusing for a little girl growing up.

I think I was right about that, but I also stayed too long in relationships for the same reason. I never let anyone move in with me – again too confusing. Although my advice to Bre after my second divorce was to live together before marrying anyone, this was a moral issue for me as well. That too was something she didn't do. She and Ben had gone together in high school and reunited as adults, so she felt she knew him already.

For me, the decision was simply to never fall in love. That seemed easier than making a third mistake, and whenever I was in "love," my judgment was clouded. Why is it that when we're in love we can't see the bold-faced truth about someone? For instance, we might tell ourselves they won't drink as much when we're married; we are building a life together and they'll want to spend that time with us. We figure drinking must just be a pastime. Whatever the issue may turn out to be, after much pain and broken promises, we finally realize that the ingredient or ingredients are not only missing, but unlikely to ever be found. And maybe, just maybe, he's happy with his life exactly the way it is! And really, it's *your* problem of denial and avoidance that most needs solving. Either way, the energy and time spent trying to change someone is energy and time that could be used in a far more productive way. In my case, with my daughter. Bre was graduating from high school just as I was ending my second marriage. Little did I know there was such precious little time left.

I was never able to give Bre the family life I grew up with and hoped to give her. When I shared this with her, she said, "Mom, we are our own family. We don't need anyone else." She was so right. After all, it was all she knew and she was fine with it. I was the one who wanted more for her, and it seemed I wasn't very good at it. That was the end of my search and the beginning of acceptance. I will cherish that day forever.

I met Les quite by accident. Some friends were going to Lake Havasu in Arizona for a long weekend. They had friends who had a vacation home there and invited me to come along. The plan was to lie around the pool and drive to Laughlin (for a little casino time) while the guys played golf. Sounded fun to me, so off we went.

The first thing we did was walk through the house to the pool. I noticed a man sitting in a deck chair, sporting a red bathing suit. He had a dark tan, black horn-rimmed glasses, silver hair, and a cigar in his hand. He looked very serious. What would you think if you saw that? I wondered if he was the Godfather himself. But no, this was Les, and much to my relief, not a godfather. In fact very much the opposite.

The weekend went as planned, with the girls doing their thing and the guys playing golf. As we were getting ready to leave for the airport, I made a comment about wearing my same old dirty jeans, while making a gesture of brushing the dirt off. You know the routine: you bring a suitcase full of clothes and end up wearing the same thing. Bre believed if it didn't fit in a backpack, you didn't need it. I never mastered packing the way she did. But then again, she traveled to Europe, with road trips to California and Georgia. She joined a travel group in Africa where a silverback gorilla charged her and a bird swooped in to steal her lunch. In Indonesia she road an elephant through a torrential down pour and a monkey jumped on her back to slap her. The world – and all its people and animals – was very important to her. She wanted to see it all. Bre had learned to travel on a shoestring, and always with a trusty backpack.

After we returned home, my friend called and asked me to meet her and her husband for dinner. Okay, sounded great, and off I went. A bit later Les walked in carrying a Nordstrom box. I was completely shocked as he handed it to me. We'd barely had a conversation all weekend and here he was, giving me a gift!? He said, "It was your birthday, wasn't it?" "Yes, but what's this for?" "Open it," he said. It was a new pair of jeans! I started laughing as he said, "I thought everyone should have, at least, *two* pair of jeans." That was how I met Les. I was 49 years old.

Bre and Les got to know each other when they planned my 50th birthday party. Bre and I shared the same birthday. What an incredible gift she was! Les said that when she sat down in the middle of the floor and surrounded herself with the various colors of paper plates, trying to decide which colors I might like, he knew he was going to have fun, and they did. That was the beginning of the close relationship that developed between my daughter and Les. I will be forever grateful for that.

The second most incredible gift came in 2005, when she and her husband Ben invited me into the birthing room as she gave birth to my little grandson, Owen. Her own little miracle. Because I was given strict instructions to be very quiet, I watched with my hands over my mouth as she brought Owen into this world. I am still overwhelmed by their generosity in sharing that moment with me.

Little did I know I would lose her in 2006. My life changed forever. I thought, *nothing is as it should be. Where is she? Will I see her again? Is God real?* When my dad left, I didn't question it. I just knew he was in heaven. After all, that was what I had been taught, so it must be true. But such assurances were no longer enough. Where was the proof? Faith would not be enough. I just knew I had to find her or I couldn't go on. What would the point of life be without my Bre? If this is all there was going to be, one painful experience after another, then nothingness would be better. I HAD TO FIND HER. And so the search began.

CHAPTER TWO

My Search Begins

Was it possible I was led to a book
written by a medium?

I awoke one morning with an overwhelming sense I should drive to the cabin. I didn't think I could ever go there again. The pain of knowing Bre would never be there was more than I could handle. It was the last place she and Ben had taken Owen. She called it their first mini family vacation. Yet here I was, feeling compelled to drive up there. What did this mean? Would I find her there? I had to go.

I arrived, opened the door, and was hit with an overwhelming sense of loss. *She's not here. Why am I here? Is there a book I should read?* We did have a few thought-provoking books there. I pulled some books down and began to read. *No, this isn't it. Oh, why am I here?* I just needed to leave. I walked back to the bookshelf and began to put them back, when I noticed a book by Sylvia Browne, *The Other Side and Back.* Sylvia was a well-known psychic and medium. I had never read that one and wasn't sure where it came from. I noticed two markers in it. The kind Bre would use (a torn sticky note). One was under children and the other under loss. I didn't know why, but I believed this was what I was meant to find.

I don't believe in magic, so I began to investigate where the book might have come from. As it turned out, Wendy ("her other mom") had given her a stack of books and that book was in it. I believe when Bre had her miscarriage, she was also looking for answers. Those particular passages must have given her some comfort. Is it possible she hoped they would help me, too? Could she actually have led me to it? It does make you wonder.

I brought it home with me and began to read. I wasn't sure why I would be led, if that's possible, to read a book written by a psychic/medium. Many religions teach us it is wrong, even though the Bible is full of prophets and seers. It's considered a sin to turn to anyone but God. Just one more question I had about the Bible.

Hell was another teaching I had a very hard time with. I couldn't imagine anything my Bre could do that would make me consider sending her – or anyone I knew – to hell. However, hell had been so ingrained into my subconscious that I was concerned. Is it possible God, Our Eternal Father, could really do that to one of His own children? I was pretty sure Bre had crossed all her t's and dotted all her i's, so I fervently hoped she was with God. But if, for some unknown reason, hell exists and she were there, I would never leave her all alone. Would you? How could God? Wherever she is, is where I want to be.

The Old Testament seemed to be full of wars, licentious/unlawful sex, and, I suppose, just good old-fashioned sin. The stories of adulterous love read like a novel written in the language of the day. In fact, one could become vicariously involved in any of those stories. But it seemed to be mainly a chronicle of ancient events, along with prophecies and an attempt to interpret what God wants of us.

Is this the word of God or the words of prophets? Prophets had the ability to see visions, hear voices, and sense spirit/God. A medium has these same abilities. I don't know when or how or by whom it was decided that some would be revered as seers, oracles, and prophets while others would be linked to witchcraft. I suppose it could have to do with jealousy, money, or fear, from all parties concerned. Where are these prophets and prophecies today? Did they disappear with the last word in the Bible? Modern-day prophets, as some would call themselves, don't seem to have the same importance that they did then.

I was taught when you are struggling with a problem, you should pray and read the Bible. The answer is there. Ah, but for the interpretation, do you trust your own ideas, or someone else's? This is why we have Bible study groups, so we can discuss these differences. Could this also be why there are so many different Christian denominations, even though they all base their belief on the Bible?

I remember a time when it was believed that if you weren't a member of the right church, you would not make it to heaven. That's an awful lot of pressure as there were many to choose from, and I'm certainly glad it's said not to matter anymore — as long as it's a Christian church. Oh, but not just *any* Christian church. One's house of worship must still embrace some very particular interpretations. But, *whose* interpretation? It's sad to me that so many people turn away from God because of these interpretations. That would never be God's intent, don't you agree?

So then, does God answer prayers in every religion — or just yours? It seems reasonable to me that He would, or you would have nothing to base your belief on. Oh, but we're told that Satan, always on the lookout to cause trouble, answers those prayers. Wow! So when I pray to God, I can't trust God is answering me? If he truly is our Father in Heaven, I think He'd just be happy I was talking to Him and not allow Satan to intercept the communication. I have to believe the omnipotent God has absolute power — including over Satan. Do you? Life is complicated enough without having to worry that when I talk to my Dad in Heaven, He would hang me out to dry with Satan, and not protect my conversation with Him.

When you read the New Testament, you will find love and forgiveness. Did God send Jesus to make that message clear? Could it be as simple as that? Jesus was not a Christian, yet who more worthy than He to be in Heaven? Jesus tore down the walls that insisted you needed an intercessor, a clergyman, to talk to God. He taught us that we can speak directly to Him ourselves, and He to us. Jesus didn't have an ego that needed strokes; he just loved God more than life itself. He wanted us to know how fully and unconditionally God loves everyone, no matter what their status, religion, or nationality. He truly is the Savior to all mankind and not a select few.

I always wondered why Jesus didn't write a book. From what we understand, He was educated in the temples. Why didn't He write something, anything? Do you suppose He did and it was destroyed? If so, why? It does make you wonder, doesn't it? And how did a peasant get into the temples to study when peasants were not allowed inside? It is believed He was a descendant of King David, so was He really a peasant? So much is simply not known about Jesus, the man.

There are ever so many unanswered questions! Human answers are simply not trustworthy enough to believe without at least some doubt. Maybe it's the message of love God is most interested in and not the details, which are so important to man. The message of LOVE seems especially hard for us to understand and embrace; otherwise, we would stop fighting over who is more righteous and "favored."

As you can see, for me, the Bible was gradually losing its credibility. Was it the absolute and final Word of God, or was it more the words of men driven by greed and their need to control? Might its authors have lost sight of God's unconditional LOVE for us and qualified it with conditions more suited to their personal gain? Is that possible?

Any religion is a beautiful thing as long as it brings you closer to God and does not separate you from anyone else. He created a masterpiece and He created it for you. It is a miracle this masterpiece exists, as your own eyes — and any scientist — will readily tell you. If you believe in God, how can you believe He would play favorites and not love *all* of His creations? Remove the ego and you will see this has to be true.

CHAPTER THREE

Psychics and Mediums

The lack of knowledge creates fear.
I needed to learn more about them.
Was that a sin?

Since I believe I was led to a book written by a medium, I wanted to learn more about them. I began reading all I could find. Leviticus 19:31 in the Old Testament says, "Do not turn to mediums." In 1 Corinthians 10:23 we're told, "Everything is permissible but not always beneficial." Knowledge is the only way to know what the benefits may be.

What is a psychic or a medium? Are they different or the same? Regardless, I believe there can be no sin in seeking knowledge, so I continued on. I started with books written by mediums, then doctors and scientists. What did they have to say about a consciousness, soul, or spirit that lives on after death? This is what I found.

A medium is someone who has the ability to see, feel, and/or hear spirit from the other side. Some people call the other side heaven, or our real home. Whatever you want to call it, I have come to believe it is where we came from and where we return to after we leave this physical plane. A medium is always psychic, but a psychic is not always a medium. A psychic is a person who has visions or dreams of things and events, beyond his physical senses, of what is to come. A medium can see and hear spirit from the other side, which allows them to hear of and see the things to come. There are also intuitives with the ability to sense things at a much deeper level than simple intuition. It would appear that they can feel and read the energy fields around them. It is not uncommon for psychics and mediums to be intuitive as well. Do you suppose the prophets of the Bible had these abilities? It seems a possible, and even logical explanation.

These fields are of course jam-packed with charlatans, not all that different from those found in religion, politics, business, etc. Their goal: personal gain. Any arena in which people can be led opens the door to greed and the egotists who appear to gain from it. Send me your money and I'll make your life better! A first class front row seat in heaven!? I believe you already have that. The more information you have about the organization or person you're giving your money to, the better.

Mediums can be as diverse in personality as any of us. Some are extroverts, who can handle criticism and don't have a problem speaking to large groups. Others prefer to work in private, staying out of the public eye. Some feel frightened or uncomfortable when contact is made, blocking their visions or the messages coming through to them. They don't see their abilities as a gift but rather as an intrusion upon their peace and privacy. Those who regard their "second sight" as a gift are in a position to help people who are suffering, and believe it their duty to use it for that purpose. There are cases of near-death experiences (NDEs) that have served to develop these abilities by seemingly opening up that aspect of the brain. That was interesting to me.

One such gifted person was a friend of mine. He came to me when my daughter left to tell me of his near-death experience. He was a young boy when he was electrocuted and, for an unmeasurable moment in (or outside of) time, he found himself somewhere he wanted to stay forever. The love he felt was like nothing he could explain or has ever felt since. It wasn't of this Earth. Because of that love, he knew with absolute certainty that it was a real place – and something he could never have imagined. Years later, he was able to meet with his parents after they had passed. They wanted him to know they were happy. What a gift! He wanted me to know

Bre was happy too, because he knew where she was. I will be forever grateful for the love people showed me during this time.

It is believed that disciplines such as meditation and visualization stimulate the area of the brain known as the pineal gland that can open to this kind of awareness. In other words, this ability is believed to be in all of us. We are spiritual beings, so that does seem possible. Some wouldn't want to try these exercises for fear they would be committing a sin. Others simply wouldn't have the discipline it takes. But many have indeed been successful in their attempts. If you are born with these abilities already open, it is far easier. Yet many don't understand or are afraid to acknowledge their gift, and there's no one around to explain it to them. It's no wonder we have let that part of our brain stay dormant or even atrophy over the centuries, as stoning and other tortures were once an accepted punishment for this insight. If you're interested in these exercises and disciplines, there are many books written on the subject.

There is one fun thing I like to do. It is an exercise my nephew does. He stands at the entrance of a trailhead and imagines what it looks like (the moss on the trees, the rock formations, a fallen tree, water, etc.). Then he walks down the trail. For many tries, nothing happened. Then miraculously, one day it was all there, just as he had envisioned. Now it seems he knows what he'll see before he walks down any trail. You can try this exercise yourself whenever you're going somewhere you've never been. I, however, am not as dedicated to these exercises as my nephew was and is, but when I think of it, I still try.

For many years, I was taught it was a sin to meditate, because meditation was considered relying on yourself and not on God for answers you are seeking. And with this belief came fear to look any further into what meditation actually is. I now understand fear is the opposite of love and God is love, so what is there to be afraid of? President Franklin D. Roosevelt's succinct answer was: "The only thing we have to fear is fear itself." Certainly God has no fear of what you read or the ideas you consider. Man might, but not God. Remember, there is no sin in knowledge, only the lack of it. I believe the lack of knowledge spawns fear, and fear stops the world and you from moving forward. Fear causes wars! Can you see that? If we don't understand something, we fear it and want to destroy it. Where is the logic in that? Meditation is simply clearing the mind to invite spirit in. You can do it while you're weeding your garden. It doesn't have to be a big production, unless you want to make it one.

Thanks to the mediums and psychics who have allowed themselves to be tested, it was discovered that their right central lobe shows more activity than is commonly seen. It therefore stands to reason that with targeted practice, you too could develop these dormant abilities. As with all exercise, the more you do, the stronger and more skillful you become. Is all of this beginning to sound a little less mystical and more like something real? As Pierre Teilhard de Chardin, a Jesuit priest, famously said, "We are not human beings having a spiritual experience. We are spiritual beings having a human experience." If so, is this our link to who we truly are?

It can't be easy being a medium. You're open to a lot of criticism and accusations. If you're born with this ability, you initially think everyone sees the same things you do. When you realize they don't, you begin to question your own sanity. It's no wonder that so many mediums are open to being tested. They want to understand where their impressions are coming from more than we do — especially if they were taught to believe they came from Satan. How sad is that?

So why don't they get their impressions and predictions right every time? A medium can be influenced by his or her own personal beliefs and filter messages through them. They try to tune them out, but it's hard to do. Again, it's a matter of interpretation. Remember they can hear, see, and/or feel the world of spirit. The more abilities they have, the more accurate the interpretation. Many mediums would prefer that you learn to open to the spirit within you yourself, and have written how-to books on the subject. They believe your interpretation is always closer to the actual message.

I don't rely on psychics, mediums, or prophets simply because I know their interpretation can be off. Here's an example. I asked a medium if she could tell me something personal that Bre and I might have shared. She said she saw her bedroom and it was full of flowers. All the walls were covered in flowers. That certainly wasn't Bre's bedroom. She liked flowers but not on her walls. Had she looked further she might have seen a cat curled up on the bed. Our cat, Flower, was especially important to Bre and me. Had I seen that vision myself, I would have known immediately what Bre wanted me to see. One more example was when a friend of mine asked a medium what her future house would look like. The medium described it as being in the country with trees around it. It had a long driveway lined with trees and flowers. The house she purchased was as described, but it was in the middle of town. Close, but not accurate. Had my friend seen the vision herself, would she have seen something else, making it more clear?

Did this medium bring me comfort? YES! She used expressions only Bre would use. In fact, it made me laugh to hear the replies to some of the questions. She told me I was reading too much and that I needed to chill with that. I didn't believe I was reading too much so I denied it, but Bre insisted that I was, and she repeated that I needed to chill. Of course, I haven't stopped reading and I'm sure Bre's fine with that. She just wanted me to know she knew. There was no doubt this medium was communicating with Bre and that Bre wanted me to know she was there. I now believe Bre is waiting for the people she loves to join her when their job here is done.

Seers, oracles, and prophets have always been around. Yet, some were persecuted or burned at the stake for being witches, while others were revered as prophets. Who decides that, and why? There are descriptions in the Bible of false prophets (Deuteronomy 18:9-22). Some of these mediums/prophets/seers were killed simply because they couldn't give the king the favorable forecast he wanted. Does that make them false prophets? A false prophet is one who tells you things that don't come true. Really? It seems centuries may go by before certain prophecies can be realized. Worse, people could actually act in ways to *make* some of them come to pass. Interpretation is everything, so unless you see it yourself, you can't be sure it's completely accurate.

Is it uncomfortable to think that religions may have started as the result of one man who believed himself a prophet with a direct pipeline to what God wanted? Did they get it right? How would they know God had spoken to them? What were their belief systems in that day? They knew little to nothing of the spirit that lives in each of us. Undoubtedly, there is room for error no matter how well-meaning they were.

It's possible that many more are born with a connection to spirit than we're aware of. A good number of children have just come from the other side, "trailing clouds of glory from God, who is our home." (William Wordsworth, "Intimidations of Immortality") Can they still see their spirit guides or angels? How many of our children had imaginary friends? Bre had two friends, Mary and Sam. I would listen to her conversations with them, assuming it was because she was an only child and needed a friend. Although I wasn't one of those parents who tell their kids they're not real, I certainly didn't believe they were. We would have little tea parties and I would even talk to them, never once believing I might actually be talking to someone. I just wish I knew then what I know now. I might have asked some questions and received some interesting answers through my daughter.

Breana used to draw a favorite picture when she was very young. She described it as being "the attic in the sky." It was always the same picture, even though it was gibberish to her dad and me. The significance it held for her I'll never know, because I didn't ask. But I did tell her how pretty it was. Fortunately, her father decided to stage an artist interview and asked the questions I didn't. He had it notarized and framed for me for Christmas. What a gift! Here is the interview. She was four years old.

On December 12th, 1980, I was commissioned by the artist, Breana McCandlis, to supervise all matting, framing, and publishing of her latest work to eventually be presented on the 25th of December, 1980, to her mother Cynthia Mae McCandlis.

This multicolor original piece in ink pen depicts the evolutionary progress of humanity. The circular purple and red areas are tomatoes. From the raw purple growing state to the fully ripened red, they symbolize the cultural growth of society. The square shapes with crossbars, the artist states, are cages representing the ever-present darker side to humanity. Significantly, the largest area of the picture is given to a recurring theme in Breana's work...the attic in the sky. When asked if "attic in the sky" was perhaps heaven, the artist's reply was yes. This brilliantly multicolored area represents the hope of the future.

Breana has surely tapped the source of her being to create her view of humanity.

Of course, most of that interview was in her father's words, but taken from her replies. Little did we know it would bring comfort to us years later. I never knew if there was an actual book *Attic in the Sky* that someone had read to her (although I found nothing in my google search) or if it was her memory of where she had come from. In either case, as I look at it, I believe it's where she is now. A place she thought was beautiful and loved to draw. I hope to visit her in her purple and red tomato garden one day. Since she liked to garden, it wouldn't surprise me to find her there.

When Bre left, her son was five months old. At times, he would lie on his back, reach for the sky, and laugh as though someone were tickling him. Anyone who saw it believed it had to be Bre playing with her baby. It was so intense that the first few times we saw him doing it, we wondered if there was something wrong with him. Sadly, as he got older, it stopped. It's interesting to think of a little baby as a highly evolved spirit inhabiting a human body, who is still able to see into another dimension. How would we treat our babies if we knew that were true? If they could talk, what would we learn? It must be shocking to transition from free movable energy to a tight restricted body in which every movement is an effort and communication is mostly verbal. No wonder so many "fussy babies" are not too happy about it at first. Physical life must be an incredible gift or we would never leave the wonderful world of energy and love.

CHAPTER FOUR

Who Is God?

He is the love and
energy of the universe.

Is He the orchestrator of the universe, the ultimate scientist, or is "He" fiction? That's a question asked by most people at some point in their life. I grew up knowing God as my Father in Heaven. I envisioned Him with white hair and a flowing beard, with Jesus at His side. He was radiant with light and very much a human man. I knew He loved me, forgave me my sins, and would protect me, because the church told me I was saved. It wasn't until I grew older and life happened that I began to truly question what that meant. Life was simpler when Santa Claus was real, but alas – he's not. So is God real, or was He invented to make life a little easier and/or to keep us in line? For me, if God is not real, then heaven isn't real either, and Bre is gone forever. Yet, I had to know, and faith was not enough.

My search for God had started years earlier. I read the Bible two times, cover to cover. I joined a Bible study group to discuss the various interpretations. I couldn't understand why my interpretation would sometimes be so very different from the minister's. He explained that he was a learned man, and that the Bible says we should accept the teachings of learned men. I didn't understand why God would write a book for all mankind if we needed others to tell us what it said.

The final break from that church and the minister, who was Lutheran, came when the sermon involved telling the congregation which religions were pagan and why their believers would be condemned to everlasting torment in hell if they didn't change their beliefs. Isn't that how wars start? I knew some of these people from other religions, and many of them were Mormons. I found them to be good people, so why would God send them to hell? I got up and left that day and never went back. I was now convinced the Bible was a little *off* – or at least this learned man's understanding of it.

One thing was certain to me: God, if He exists at all, would have to have been here long before any religion. There was no fitting God into any one box. The ubiquitous One would be both inside and outside the box. And what is God's favored religion? Is He a Jewish god, a Muslim god, a Christian god, etc.? How about Baha'i? Does His approval extend to all the different denominations within these core religions? Every religion presumes to know exactly what God wants. It's not logical God would put these labels on Himself. We did that. He has to be a God of love and unity, not division. This world with everything in and around it doesn't make sense any other way. Everything has to work together.

Needless to say, I stopped searching any further. I couldn't come to terms with anything I was being told, and formed my own idea of what God is. It wasn't until I lost Bre and became desperate to find her that my search resumed in earnest. If this is all there is, then what are we living this crazy, sad life for? Through this process, I began to think about life differently. All the roads I went down took me to more roads I could never have foreseen. That journey took me to a truly loving God, and to my Bre.

The stories in the Bible seem to give God human characteristics. This anthropomorphic God is jealous, wrathful, vengeful, and with a big ego who is always testing your faith. He commands the destruction of whole nations if its inhabitants are not meticulously following His laws. I had a problem with that, as many of us do. If such a being as God exists, how could he be so insecure and cruel? And He would hardly be a king, sitting passively on a throne, which was how many seemed to view Him. He wouldn't NEED us for anything, including our adoration or obedience. He already has, and is, everything.

The Bible also speaks of a loving God. That seems incongruous with a God who condemns us for not believing in Him and His laws. So, which is it? Are we to fear God or to love God? Does He send us, His children, to hell to be punished for all eternity, or does He love us unconditionally? How can He be both?

What did we know about the paranormal – or even the normal – centuries ago? Surely our forebears witnessed their share of mysterious and fearsome natural and supernatural phenomena. Were gods and goddesses created in an effort to explain them, along with our very existence? It seems that deities have been around since the dawn of mankind. Is it possible we misused the Ultimate Reality and instead used it as a tool to advance our personal agendas? Great way to get people to do one's bidding! Heads of church and state could easily manipulate the masses into believing they were carrying out God's will, and not their own. It's no wonder so many people turned agnostic or even atheistic. God was seen as the image and likeness of man, rather than the other way around. He was portrayed as a vulnerable human, with human weaknesses and strengths, which He most assuredly is not!

I don't believe God is a supernatural, magical being. He is, rather, the ultimate scientist, the creator and sustainer of all that we see and don't see. The One who knows – and is – all that there is to know. Science is trying to figure out how it all came into being, they just don't know that it's *Him* they're trying to figure out. The quantum world is an invisible realm wherein our thoughts affect all the energy that's out there (and in here). This is God's world, and it is a mystery to the greatest sage or scientist. I sometimes wonder what would happen if scientists did not equate God with religion. Would they look more closely at the consciousness that underlies and orchestrates all that energy out there? In fact, could God be the very energy that we call the quantum world and not an individual entity?

In the scientific community, reference is sometimes made to an intelligent designer. It's hard to describe the quantum world without the possibility of thought behind it. An intelligence that, with the creative power of thought, starts and sustains everything. Could it be that we, created in His image, hold that same power? Jesus is said to have said: "The works that I do shall you do also, and greater works." (John 14:12) Did Jesus understand the "mechanics" of God's universe and the power the mind has on it? Unlike mediums, who are in contact with spirit guides, Jesus was said to be in direct contact with God, fully aware of His unity with Him, and was thought by many to be God Himself in human form. Did He perform miracles that He could not understand? Or might He have had a complete understanding of God's creation and how it all works?

We'll look more closely at the quantum world in another chapter, but for now, here's a peek at what I believe God's world might look like. Simply defined, a proton is a subatomic particle. When you separate two protons, regardless of how far apart, they remain in communication, responding to each other. Einstein called this phenomenon "spooky action at a distance." In other words, they are still connected – somehow "entangled," as physicists would say. At one time, all protons were believed to have been compressed to a size smaller than a pea, burning at 18 billion million million million degrees F (give or take a degree) that simply exploded, enabling all of life and matter to evolve. At one time, everything was connected. God then contracted and God expanded – He breathed in and He breathed out. Maybe. If He were the Big Bang, it would explain how we are made in His image, or at least of the same stuff as He – He, a part of us, and we, a part of Him. It would also explain how He so intimately knows what's in our hearts, and how it could be true that we are all one Being. He is everywhere, in and as everything. He is not loftily or remotely "up there" and we somehow "down here." Is this what Jesus actually meant when He said, "I and my Father are One" (John 10:30) or "Whoever has seen me has seen the Father"? (John 14:9) Just a thought.

It is estimated that the universe is some 93 billion light-years across. A light-year is the distance light travels in a year. Light travels at 186,000 miles per second and a year has 31,556,926 seconds. Care to do the math? And within that space, there are at least 200 billion galaxies. Then again, the number of galaxies may be infinite. No one knows for certain. If the universe is a bubble, then how many bubbles might there be? It's said that space and time have no utility or meaning in God's world, so what was there before our universe was formed? Unimaginable! How small and insignificant I appear to be! Yet to God, I am of utmost significance. That's because at one "time," we were all one and I believe we still are. The separation is an illusion. Impossible for the mind to even imagine it.

Does God have a name? Yes, many names, and whatever your religion has chosen to give Him it is the right name. I cannot imagine it would matter to God what you call Him. No name can do Him justice. The name God seems almost mythical, like Zeus or Hera. He wants your love, not your fear of Him. If calling Him Charley makes you feel closer to Him, I'm sure He would be fine with that. In fact, in the unlikely event that He has preferences, He might like that name better than some of the other names people have given Him over the centuries.

"Ehyeh-Asher Ehyeh," it is said, is how He defined Himself to Moses, and translates loosely as "I am that I am." The name He actually went by with Moses was YHWH, pronounced Yahweh. We have to take Moses's word for it, as there were no witnesses, but let's assume it's true. Yahweh is the oldest recorded name for the biblical God, but scholars are not sure of the actual vowels in the translation because there were no vowels given. It was commonly held that to mispronounce His holy name was disrespectful, so only the high priests were allowed to speak it. Considering that the pronunciation is somewhat of a guess, I believe God is not as vested in His name as we are. If He were, I believe He would have been much clearer about it. He *is* God, after all, and I don't think it would have been a problem for Him to get His point across. "I am that I am" is a concept that defines Him. The name is merely a word.

I hope this doesn't sound disrespectful because I know He loves us, *all* of us, more than we can understand. The name doesn't explain or describe the One Presence. It's just the tip of the iceberg. So as we struggle with things that seem important to us, like His name, His all-inclusive sound is the message of LOVE. Will we ever hear it?

Many are taught that God will judge us in the end, with the majority being dispatched to hell for an eternity of unrelenting torment. If God loves us unconditionally, then what might He be judging? So, which is it – a loving God or a vengeful, judging, punishing God? Fundamentalist Christians are satisfied with the explanation that while God is all-merciful and all-loving, He is also all-righteous. In any case, punishment for all eternity seems excessive. I wouldn't wish it on my worst enemy! A much more reasonable scenario is that *we judge ourselves* under the guardianship of the all-loving God. At least, this is what some who have experienced NDEs (near-death experiences) seem to experience, following a lifetime review.

A God of love doesn't cause bad things to happen. It is we ourselves, or other humans who are usually at the cause of it. To learn and to grow from the incessant experiences of life is why we chose to come here and the reason this "here" was created. Some people believe God is "testing their faith" when things are going badly for them. I don't believe God toys with us that way, nor that He would need to administer a test to see into our already transparent hearts. I believe it's our love that He seeks, and that this is what Jesus taught. We have come to learn in an environment that includes negative energy in it, unlike Heaven where love is all there is. Bad things have and will continue to happen; God has nothing to do with it. It's an essential part of the journey we signed up for. The choice to come here was ours to make, and we are here now, ready to meet the challenges to the best of our ability.

Along with the idea of God "testing" people, many also believe that when they become seriously ill, He is punishing them for some transgression or another. Maybe they got this idea from the Bible verse, "Sin no more, lest a worse thing come unto you." (John 15:14). Even deformities have been thought to be caused by sin. Early man knew nothing about germs or genes. I think that verse may be referring to the universal law of attraction, having nothing to do with punishment: *Good attracts good and bad attracts bad.* Notice that the verse doesn't say God will do it: it says sin will do it. "You reap what you sow." If you project happiness, more happiness comes your way, and if you project anger, more things to be angry about come your way. As I said earlier, Jesus seemed to know how the universe worked, and I think He tried to teach us.

Did you know the word sin was translated from the Greek word *hamartia*? It means, to miss the mark or to miss the target. It's used in the Bible to mean transgressions against God, yet that's not the actual translation. Maybe we missed the mark on what it was actually meant to signify. Just thought you should know this.

I liked this statement in Ernest Holmes's book *The Hidden Power of the Bible.* "We are surrounded by a Universal Law, which is entirely impartial, and which returns to the thinker the logical effect of his actions. Man, being a free agent in this law – whether consciously or in ignorance – is continually setting it in motion to some definite end. Therefore it is true, unalterably true, that *he must reap as he has sown.*" God created a universe that brings you your heart's desires, so be very aware and careful about what's really in your heart.

We have a tendency to look at other people's lives and wonder how such a mean and undeserving person can seem to be having a good life. That "you reap what you sow" doesn't seem to apply to them. The thing is, you really don't know much about the journey they're on. I know each person I meet is having his or her own experience, and it's not for me to judge or speculate. Ultimately, it is their own life and experience. I have enough to concern myself with in my own life as I try to give my best to God.

Is there a Devil? I personally don't believe that Satan is an actual being. It's said there is no negative energy in heaven, yet we seem to have a lot of it here. Why is that? Could Satan or the Devil be not a discrete entity but rather a name given to this negative energy? Temptation to harm self or others arises out of that energy. Without it, there would be nothing to learn and no choices to make. Wisdom can be gained only through the ramifications of each choice. Whether the experience feels good or bad, happy or sad, it is just what it is, an experience. We actually need the negativity or "Devil" in order to have a choice to make. "The Devil made me do it!" No, he did not. The temptation arose and you made the choice. We are spirit, which is eternal. The human experience goes away, but the wisdom gained from each choice is ours for eternity. We will return home and leave this life behind. God gave us this opportunity. He certainly didn't have to, but we wanted the experience of choice which required a negative environment. That is unconditional love, and that is what God is.

What about angels? Do they exist? If so, what are they? Some believe angels were created before human beings while others believe they came after. In either case, they were created to watch over us. They have never lived a human, physical life. They have no gender and can appear in any form that the situation requires. I often wonder why anything bad happens when we have such powerful beings around us. It's believed we have a mission/purpose, and that angelic intervention cannot disrupt the natural order of that mission. It's also possible that they might be waiting in the wings to be asked, and we simply don't ask. Some people say they have had angel encounters, and it's possible that some have had them and not been aware of it. It's a mystery to me, but I'd like to think they're real. Many books are written on the subject of angels. I liked *Book of Angels* by Sylvia Browne. Her interpretation of them and the way she describes their power and beauty was encouraging to me.

Is God male, female, both, or something else altogether? In the earliest texts, God was not referred to as either he or she, but was one of non-gender. In other words, "He" means "It." Absent any word for that, "He" was adopted. In the book of Genesis, it is written that God created humanity in His own image: "Let us make man in our image, after our likeness." Who is "us" and to whom does "our" refer? He created a world of duality, so it seems there is an argument for both. A mother god to nurture and a father god to keep things in order. Or perhaps He is both in one. But it doesn't really matter either way, as love is all that matters. We have to remember LOVE and stop casting stones. As I've said earlier, God has no ego, so however you choose to know Him, I'm sure He will love you just the same. Or is it She?

It's as though God is hardwired somewhere in our subconscious. Religions try to describe and define Him, but I believe we're moving closer to who God is and to acknowledging His ubiquity through science. The invisible world of atoms may hold the answer. The world of matter is the real illusion. It's just a bunch of atoms clumped together to form something that appears solid. Our soul, spirit, or consciousness evolves from what we experience on Earth and is eternal, just as He is. Our human life ends.

I am going to close this chapter by simply saying He is the energy of the universe and beyond—GOD IS LOVE. He can't be anything else. As my friend who had an NDE told me, "It is a love I have never experienced as a human being. That's how I know what I experienced was real. I didn't want to leave."

Unconditional, completely consuming LOVE. He like a good Father, always here and always there, waiting for you, now and forever.

CHAPTER FIVE

Science and Quantum Theory

The more we understand the quantum
nature of the physical world, the closer
God and science become.

When I began looking at quantum theory, I hoped to zero in on a simple explanation. Had I known anything about the quantum world, I'd have known how ridiculous that was.

Years ago, we assumed the universe stood still. It had objects in it, surrounded by empty space. Now we know it's very much alive and ever-expanding. Stars are exploding, galaxies forming, and everything is comprised of various states of energy. There is no empty space. Using mathematics in the mid-1600s to model the physical world, Newton laid the foundations for quantum mechanics. He proposed an "invisible" force called gravity, and that objects with mass have a gravitational pull on other objects with mass. To some, this meant that the universe is held together by this invisible force called gravity, and not by God. Many cried "blasphemy!" How can something invisible have any power at all? He must have seemed a bit eccentric, even heretical — a very scary and endangered figure to cut in that day — until his theories were proven through mathematics to be correct.

Early man turned his gaze upward for answers, up to the stars of the night sky. Then came sacred writings and religion to explain life, and now we have science and mathematics, which is where I believe the answers are. Sadly, God was seen as incompatible with science, and got thrown out with the bathwater of religion. I believe He is the energy of the universe, the ultimate scientist, the original mathematician, and the mastermind behind our existence.

It was soon obvious that the mathematics of classical physics could not be employed to predict anything in this enormous and invisible world of energy. There were no clumps of matter to base their calculations on, nor was there any gravity. This meant new mathematical formulas had to be developed, with quantum physics resulting. The calculations involved in the new physics have thus far proven to be correct. However, with each calculation, more questions arise. The world of energy is still very much a mystery.

Science believed 90% of space was empty, leaving the 10% that we can actually see as solid. Now we know that empty space is not empty at all, but is actually energy (waves and particles), and that this energy has existed from time immemorial. Stranger than that, our thoughts seem to affect this energy field. The universe is connected via energy, not dotted by discrete pieces of matter, as we once thought. It is one living, breathing entity.

Waves and particles fill the universe. A wave is an intangible field of probabilities (ideas, thoughts, impressions). All matter and energy arise from this intangible field. A particle is matter. Unobserved, it's a wave (ideas, thoughts), flitting every which way, but when you look, it changes into particles. In other words, upon being noticed, it becomes something we consider real, or tangible. We can surmise that the real (seen and known) world could not exist without the invisible world. If that sounds confusing to you, join the club — it confuses scientists to this day. While mathematics consistently confirms that this unseen world exists, it has yet to be explained. Without factoring in superconsciousness, it may never be understood. And if consciousness is indeed what drives the subatomic world, what kind of consciousness could create all this, and whose thought would that be before the advent of man?

According to Albert Einstein, "Everyone who is seriously involved in the pursuit of science becomes convinced that a spirit is manifest in the laws of the universe — a spirit vastly superior to that of man." Another was, "I see a pattern but my imagination cannot picture the maker of the pattern...we all dance to a mysterious tune, intoned in the distance by an invisible piper." Einstein was among those who recognized the likelihood of a superconsciousness.

The atom was proven mathematically in 1913. It is less than 2 billionths of an inch in diameter and has never been seen. The atom is surrounded by empty space, and within the atom as well, more empty space. Just as in all space, the empty space isn't empty but full of even smaller things than the atom. Again, it's something we can't see, but is proven by quantum physics to exist. Remember the diagram you memorized in school of the atom? Come to find out, it was only a guess, and may not look like that at all. Who knows, maybe by the time you read this book, technology will have advanced to allow for their debut. That day will be exciting.

By itself, an atom is just an atom, but clump them together and surround them with an energy field and you have all that you can perceive. Your hand and your body would simply pass right through the wall, or your seat, were it not for the energy field around it. So how real are we, anyway? In fact, is anything solid really real? Einstein was quoted as saying, "Reality is merely an illusion, albeit a very persistent one."

Einstein's approach to the Great Mysterium was to mesh quantum physics with classical physics. Today this is called The Unified Theory. What is the missing link that surely connects them? Matter would not manifest without this invisible world.

There cannot be two separate worlds; each needs the other. They must connect somehow. A master consciousness is the logical answer, but it is very hard to prove mathematically. We need to distinguish this master consciousness from religion before science will give serious thought to its existence.

Einstein's famous equation E= **mc²,** was a huge breakthrough in science. He proved energy is equivalent to mass times the speed of light squared. In other words, energy and mass or matter are the same thing. One is just moving faster than the other. Matter and energy are completely entangled, making the universe and everything in it (including us) one big living breathing organism. Doesn't that dovetail with the mystical knowing that "we are all one with God," and Jesus' statement in the Gospel of Thomas that "The kingdom of God is inside of you, and it is outside of you?" Was He trying to give us The Unified Theory?

Many believe that plants are a sentient part of this one living breathing organism. The "Backster Effect" was the surprising result of polygraph tests performed on plants to see if they can feel empathy for other plants. It appears that they do. If you burn a leaf – even the leaf of one of the tested plant's friends – does it feel it, or at least register distress? According to Cleve Backster, it does. In fact, at the mere *thought* of harming a plant or any of its associates, Backster recorded similarly strong responses, suggesting telepathic awareness to human intentions. It appears all living things are connected at some level, no matter how far apart they are from one another. So, do our thoughts, words, and deeds affect the world around us? It appears to be true. As the events of 9/11 unfolded, there was a change in the electromagnetic field of the Earth. As Gregg Braden said in his book *The Spontaneous Healing of Belief*, "The whole world was in mourning and it felt it." This can happen only if things are connected somehow.

Since the coming of man, there have been gods and goddesses to answer the questions of creation. Why would these feared deities, who place great emphasis on punishing and rewarding you for your deeds, create all of this, and then give you the power to create as well? Why, indeed? If our existence is an accident, why does our consciousness play a presumably leading role in the quantum world of waves and particles? Science uses math and avoids the possibility of a god, especially the god whose followers tortured and imprisoned their fellow scientists for heresy. Mainstream science doesn't want to recognize a "god in the machine," and you can hardly blame them. But what would happen if they did?

In 1944, Max Planck (whom some consider the father of quantum theory) stated: "There is a 'matrix' of energy that provides the blueprint for our physical world." He believed in the possibility of a conscious, intelligent mind behind this matrix of energy. What name would you give this matrix of energy? Universal Intelligence, the Creator, Superconsciousness? Many scientists do recognize the possibility of an orchestrator of some kind, but would not want to name it God. I'm afraid religion, which man created, did more harm to God's reputation – our understanding of "His" intentions – than good.

Inspired by the mysteries of this invisible world, the scientific community gathers in conferences around the world to put forth and discuss theories, with the hope of proving some of them. When interpretations are based on the prejudicial nature of individual perception, progress moves slowly, impeded by ego. It's interesting the way Bible study groups are marked by the same dynamic, as individual interpretations on what is written are always up for debate.

Science is based on fact and driven by an unquenchable thirst to disprove or prove whatever theory is presented. Religion is based on faith, and many assumptions that can't be proven are accepted as fact. The more faith you have, the more righteous you're considered to be. Science has discovered a world of particles, particles that are affected by our thoughts. I think the word faith has far more meaning than we can imagine. Jesus said, "If you have faith as small as a mustard seed, you can say to this mountain, 'Move from here to there,' and it will move. Nothing will be impossible for you." (Luke 17:6) Did Jesus have a complete understanding of the universe God created? In other words, if we have faith, or believe what we are thinking, will it happen? Will the universe respond to our thoughts? Is that what prayer is all about – having the faith that your prayer will be answered? Is this the science behind prayer? Could it even be the science behind miracles? Has God created a universe that responds to your thoughts and answers prayer? If that's the case, as the old adage warns, "be careful what you wish for," and the feelings you put behind it.

The more we understand the quantum nature of the physical world, the more complementary do science and God seem to be. The world has become a safer place for a plurality of viewpoints now, where all sides can come together in open dialogue without fear of prison or worse. The bottom line is that we all want to know and understand the truth. Where did we come from, what are we here for, and where are we going when our life ends? Into nothingness, or into a greater consciousness?

References to the power of thought were edited out of the Bible in the 4th century. Why? Religious leaders believed people needed to put their trust in God alone – with them as intermediaries, of course – and not in themselves. They didn't recognize that God gave us our reasoning power to be used. Maybe they were sincere, but as self-proclaimed pipelines between God and man – the only ones who could tell you what God really wanted – heads of church and state had a great deal of power, which is never good. They pretty much ruled men and government. No one was allowed to challenge their authority without terrible consequences. Allowing dissent would be of no benefit to them or their goals. Is it possible that there were some truths in the ancient manuscripts that were excised or lost in translation, simply because their scribes and final arbiters could not understand them? Religious leaders had almost no knowledge of science at the time. If we were to translate those writings today, might we have more answers? Absent the superstitions of yesteryear, our interpretations would certainly be more illuminating.

Most of us base our beliefs on all that we learned as children from teachers, parents, peers, culture, religion, etc. Many of those fundamental assumptions may not be as true as we think. Keep your heart and mind open to new ideas! We're here to be lifetime learners. Don't close up shop and stop learning simply because a loved one or authority figure tells you "This is the way it is," or "It's a sin to look further." I liked this thought from Søren Kierkegaard [1813-1855]:

"There are two ways to be fooled. One is to believe what isn't true; the other is to refuse to believe what is true."

Science changes every day when a new truth comes to light. As technology advances, science will continue to analyze new information, proving and disproving what we believed to be true. We may be slow to accept these new truths, but eventually the textbooks change. After all, a truth is a truth. Thankfully, religion has also changed over the years and we're no longer tortured and killed for what we say, read, or believe. Of course, that's not yet the case in all parts of the world. When man can use it for power, they will. Will we ever see the truth in that?

Is it possible we have always existed in energy form, even outside of time and "before" the physical world was created? Did the human body crawl out of the sea, or did God make us from dust? And let's not forget "woman:" Was Eve born of Adam's rib? Many religions have their own elaborate stories as to our creation. I think our ego tells us we're way too special to have been generated from such seemly low materials as swamp scum. We must have been created separately, and without evolutionary input, because we're so special. Some believe it was asteroids colliding with Earth that brought the life-giving minerals. If so, everything is made of stardust or, you could say, dirt. But does it really matter? Either way, we are here, and it is nothing short of a miracle.

You look at your body and you say, "This is me." Is it? Body and brain are matter, and we all know what happens to matter. The consciousness, which drives the brain, is energy. And since energy cannot be created or destroyed, does the consciousness go on forever? Is consciousness who you truly are? Is consciousness the same as soul or spirit? Is it primary? That is the question.

Can the body survive without consciousness? It appears it can breathe and digest, etc., via instinct alone, and that consciousness brings awareness, compassion, and the ability to love. Does our spirit, soul, or consciousness simply take up residence in a body that already exists in physical form? That would mean we are two separate entities. And that's almost too weird to think about. But asking weird questions is how mysteries get solved.

One view of consciousness is that it is both within and outside of the brain – or nonlocal, which means it's everywhere. Accepting discrete soul and ubiquitous consciousness as the very same reality would be hard for some, because if individual consciousness survives death, it would suggest immortality. Such a notion borders on religious and spiritual beliefs, which tend to slow things down in the scientific community. I believe life would seem more purposeful if we knew we were consciousness, which continues on, rather than simply humans, who cease to exist. However, whenever something can't be explained, it's stored away, until someone decides to look again. In the final analysis, science wants to know the truth, so this is one of those conundrums that gets looked at often, then put aside again and again. Again I must say that if we could only separate our openness to God from our ideas about "Him," and religion, the answers would begin to come.

Some people believe that individual consciousness goes back into the invisible world of waves and particles (energy), whence it may be used to grow a tree, make a new baby, etc. Some believe it ceases to exist, snuffed into nothingness, while others have faith that it enters an afterlife of sorts. Round and round we go! According to the near-death experiences I've researched, it is our consciousness – and all that it has learned – that goes on forever. What do you think? It seems to me that there are too many similarities between the observations of near-death experiencers and the information from mediums for there not to be some truth in it. The principle of Occam's razor, as explained by author Bruce Lipton, may apply here: "When several hypotheses are offered to explain a phenomenon, the simplest hypothesis that accounts for most of the observations is the most likely hypothesis and should be considered first."

Another major mystery is time. What is time? Does it exist independently, or was it created? Without time, would we be able to experience a physical life? Einstein was fascinated with time. Can you go back in time? What about forward? People who've had NDEs say time doesn't exist in that plane. Time seems to have a different meaning in the world of energy, where past, present, and future happen all at once. Really? If this one question could be answered or even understood, would it explain who we truly are? Science has barely touched the tip of the iceberg. Where will we go from here?

Look at how far we've come since my grandparents' day, the late 19th century. My grandfather had a horse; I have a car. We have airplanes that fly great distances on currents of air. We can speak to people just about anywhere in the world without the use of wires. We discovered DNA, the code to life itself. There is little need for bookshelves as we can store whole libraries on a microchip. We can grow organs from our own cells. Our cell phone is a mini computer, with all the information we might want at our fingertips. The computer my dad used at Boeing was as big as a room. I'm sure you can add more to this list. The impossible no longer feels impossible, and technology is moving faster and faster.

We have the ability to communicate, to have feelings and ideas that shape our behavior. Are humans still evolving into something better than their human selves of today? How many thousands of years will it take before "enlightened" humanity is realized? Or will it be quicker? Will there be some huge breakthrough or catastrophe that will knock us off the merry-go-round we're on? Science is moving at a dizzying clip and becoming increasingly open to new ideas. Every time an accepted "truth" is disproven, another door opens. I believe one day we will be able to pull these unsolved mysteries out of the warehouse and integrate them into what we know of science today. That invisible world, where all things are possible, will receive them seamlessly.

My daughter, Bre, had an open and very curious mind. She would ask the questions, lots of questions, and love the discussions that followed. It's that curiosity that makes all scientists, scientists. How much fun it would have been to discuss with her some of my more recent discoveries.

CHAPTER SIX

Defining Spirituality

It's a knowing that you and everyone
else are eternal and life is a gift.

In Sylvia Browne's book, *The Other Side and Back,* she writes: "It's about the magic and miracles and support from the other side that are always around you, just waiting for you to learn how to notice them. It's about never again feeling alone or helpless or without value." This is the book I was led to read in the beginning and what started my journey to the discovery of eternity and where Bre is.

Spiritualism is not a religion. It is the knowing that we are eternal. Spiritualism lives in all of us. We just need to look and listen. We've come here for a very short time to learn; then we return with all the knowledge and experience we gained here. Spiritualists believe in the oneness of all beings. They believe God loves us just as we are, and that there's nothing to prove. They recognize love as the universal language and attempt to live their lives expressing that love.

Religion comes from the outside in, whereas spiritualism is more inwardly based. Claiming to have the one and only truth, many religions show various degrees of urgency to spread that truth to everyone else. And it is those ironclad beliefs that cause division between people, in some cases leading to martyrdom. Spiritual people feel no need to defend their differences in belief, because there's nothing to defend. We're all here for the same reason, to grow and learn. The path you choose for that learning is one of personal growth and not for others to judge. We are all one, and part of the same energy, regardless of our beliefs or the path we choose to walk. Remember, everything started with the Big Bang – one energy.

I was raised in the Church of Jesus Christ of Latter-day Saints (Mormon). It's a very family-oriented church, offering many activities for families to come together and have fun. The church has its own welfare system, including farms where food is grown to feed the needy of the church. Mormons believe in obeying the laws of the land – otherwise, polygamy would still be practiced. There are many good traditions within the church, as well as strange traditions, as is true of most religions. I, however, don't feel the need to belong to any particular religion in order to talk to God or to feel close to Him. Because He is everywhere and in everything, the only true religion is LOVE. I can't say that enough.

I wondered why this world was created in the first place. Descriptions of where we came from seemed pretty nice. We had everything, we were always loved and never alone. What more could we want? Might it be that experience in an environment that allowed negativity would enable us to embody and actually become the true meaning of empathy and compassion? We really couldn't understand pain unless we felt pain, and in our original home, there is no pain. Having the knowledge of pain is very different from experiencing pain. So, life must only be about experience and how you choose to react to it.

Some spiritualists believe we continuously evolve through many lifetimes, with the goal of returning to universal consciousness. Sometimes it does seem impossible to achieve everything in one lifetime. People with severe mental illness, or who suffered physical abuse and neglect or wartime trauma, may not have the ability to make healthy conscious decisions. What happens to them? Is it possible they have come to teach, rather than learn, in this particular life? Could they have already lived many lives? Past-life regression seems to indicate this is a possibility. Can you even allow yourself to think about that?

You can live your life with hate, anger, jealousy, revenge, etc., or in gratitude, forgiveness, and love. You can tell by the way those words feel which choices will give you a better life. The choice is yours, because whichever way you choose to live your life, you will learn. No one forced you to come here. It's how you've chosen to live your life that will make all the difference when you leave this life. A spiritual person has this understanding. I'm not saying it's always easy to choose the good feeling or the kindest response, but having the knowledge is a reminder of how to live a more peaceful life.

Deep inside all of us, is the need to be loved. If we don't get it, we go looking for it, often "in all the wrong places" and in the form of money, power, empty sex, and possessions. A spiritual person already knows that he or she is loved, deeply and unconditionally. They could have all those "things" – or not. This is why we often find spiritual masters living in caves, huts or other simple settings. Their needs are few — if any. They know who they truly are with or without them — an eternal being who is deeply loved.

You are worthy, valuable, and have a purpose. You don't even have to know what that purpose is to fulfill it. We spend far too much time wondering "What is my purpose?" Just live your life to the fullest, with integrity and compassion, and your purpose will unfold as it should.

Let go of your fear and let life happen. Learn from each experience, good or bad. We tend to be afraid of what life might bring us. How many times do you say to yourself, "Don't let this or that happen!" Life will happen no matter how hard you fight it. Whatever happens, what did you learn? Maybe the experience of this or that was your purpose. As I said, way too much time and attention is given to brooding over "What's my purpose?" "What is my special talent?" Don't let your ego tell you your purpose is to do or be something great. For all you know, what just happened a moment ago was great to your spirit.

It is great sorrow or catastrophe that causes you to re-look at your life. There is no doubt your values will change. You can choose to be sad and angry, which stops all movement, or you can try to find a reason to keep living. Even when no possible reason can be found, you need to move, just move. This is not all there is. This is a speck of time in all eternity. Knowing that has enabled me to go on without my Bre. I look forward to the time I see her again and can ask, "Just what was *that* all about? We all needed you so much." Until then, I'll keep moving forward; there's no other way.

A spiritual person is aware of the power that is around them and runs through them, and they know they can tap into it. That power, which is far beyond our understanding, is God. How much more power could you want in your corner? Our problem is that we don't always believe or have trust in that power. When you do understand its perfectly loving intentions toward you, everything changes. However, you first have to get to know Him so start talking to Him. Nothing elaborate – just talk.

What happens when you die? Some NDE people say their whole life passed before them in the blink of an eye. It seems there is an evaluation or life review, not to punish, but to teach. You'll see things you weren't aware of. The kind word at the right time to the person who needed it most, as well as the cross word at the worst time. You'll have complete understanding of all the choices you've made and how they affected you and all others. You may set some new goals and choose to come back again, or you may choose to stay. You have hundreds of thousands of years to decide. Or if you need a little more time, you have eternity.

Do truly evil people have a life review? If they choose not to go to the light, do they remain in a very dark place that some people call hell, until they "see the light?" From what I've read, there does seem to be a place of dark, negative energy between here and "the light." I'm speaking about the light at the end of the tunnel that so many near-death people have claimed to see. It seems logical to me that this is hell, chosen over the light due to dark choices on Earth. Will one stay there forever? It seems it's a choice. Would you ever choose to experience the pain and suffering you caused others, as revealed in a life review? Everything about life seems to be a choice.

Some believe that the life they've chosen to live here is the reality they will continue to live in for all eternity. Loving people go to the light, hateful people stay in the dark. It could be that simple, but I believe we always have a choice, since life without choice seems like a contradiction in terms – an oxymoron. Nothing in life stands still, nothing is constant or fixed, so how or why would one's fate be sealed? What do you think?

It's hard to go beyond what we've been told and taught over the years and look at possibilities that are completely foreign – even blasphemous to some. Yet, I'm asking you to not be afraid. Just consider it for a moment. That's what this book is about – thinking. And it's no sin to think. God has already forgiven you. I asked Him to send a bolt of lightning to change the direction of my journey if I was wrong in my quest to find Bre. God is far more loving – infinitely – than we can ever imagine, and He has allowed my journey to continue. He wasn't afraid of what I might find. In fact, I found a truly loving God – not one to be feared.

"Imagine the universe created out of love for us. Religion out of love of the creator, and science out of the love of the mystery of it all." That's just one of Dr. Fred Alan Wolf's "big ideas" in his book, *Dr. Quantum's Little Book of Big Ideas.* Do you notice the correlation in the word love in each segment?

For me, spiritualism is more of a feeling that is always within me. It doesn't matter what religion you practice or if you practice at all. It's a knowing you are eternal, along with everyone else. You have a sense of belonging to the whole human race. You are not your body, but live within that body. You are spirit and body merged into one. You are, and always have been, and always will be. The bad is not bad; the good is not good. It just is. You know God is an ever- present reality with limitless compassion, and life is a gift you don't want to waste.

I wanted to find Bre through science. Something offering facts. It led me to God, and for that there are no proven scientific facts – just a lot of evidence. In fact, I found such an abundance of evidence that it became fact for me. And where God is, Bre is, and someday I'll be there too.

CHAPTER SEVEN

Religion

Today we have many religions
and most with a prophet who received a
message from God. How confusing is that?

There was a group of men in the fourth century that decided which books would "make the cut" and remain in the Bible, and which would be deleted. I doubt that God is responsible for the finished product. At the time, there were many conflicting beliefs within the Christian faith. These men were chosen from among those holding a diversity of beliefs by the Emperor Constantine to create one Christian faith. He wanted the fighting to stop and uniformity to begin.

Where did these ancient scripts come from? It seems that cavemen practiced a burial ceremony of sorts, so maybe they were expressions of ancient beliefs. Before written language, it's likely that beliefs and stories were passed down, via the oral tradition, which eventually became books. I believe otherworldly experiences also occurred then. Absent their comprehension of such events, it would be easy to understand how a god would have been attributed to them. And a god would have rules, wouldn't he? The rules came through prophets. Prophets claimed to have received divine messages from God. To enforce these rules, fear was introduced. Punishment and the prospect of hell and purgatory became the power behind the rules. Now, that's true cower-power, useful in effecting both truly good things and truly bad things. Might religion have started this way?

Not long after 9/11, prominent atheist and evolutionary biologist Richard Dawkins opined: "Revealed faith is not harmless nonsense, it can be lethally dangerous nonsense. Dangerous because it gives people unshakable confidence in their own righteousness."

It is radical beliefs and fearful people that give religion a bad name. Inside every religion there are beautiful beliefs and wonderful, loving people. If you feel peace, harmony, and joy in your beliefs, hold on to them. If you feel the need to judge, setting yourself above others, there is no beauty in that. Anger, sadness, and separation are the results, and that's nothing to hold on to.

I have heard people say religious beliefs cause war. Religion may be an excuse for war, but not the cause. Do you suppose if religion were banned, war would cease to exist? I imagine we would find another venue to show our superiority, and capture more land and/or resources. Unless we evolve beyond those weaknesses that drive us (greed, envy, power), I can't see "peace on Earth" anytime soon. There will always be an excuse for war.

God has been the scapegoat long enough. God created human beings and gave them the free will and power to choose between good and evil, right and wrong. Good feels right and evil feels wrong. Am I right? One is godly and the other is ungodly. It really has nothing to do with religion or God. Everything is and always has been a choice. Man's choice.

All religions came into being because one person declared, with impressive authority, "I have a direct line to the divine and this is what we are to believe." The more charisma they have, the more followers they get, and just like that, a religion is born. Why can't we just believe in the freedom of love-informed choice? God created all of mankind. Why wouldn't He love all of His creation? I can't see how He could be vested in any one religion, because He didn't create religion. A man, or sometimes a woman, with a divine message did that. I repeat, it's time we stop putting God in a little box. He stands outside of the box and always has.

It's a good idea to question everything that's exterior to oneself – religious dogma, a politician, commercials, psychics, friends, family members, etc. As Socrates pointed out, and many after him have discovered, "The highest form of human intelligence is to question oneself and others." Doubt makes us think, and that's a good thing. Some religions defensively fear our asking too many questions, befriending people of other religions, and especially marrying outside the faith. Basically, anything that might draw us away from their religion is regarded with suspicion and dread. Not too long ago, the Catholic Church considered it a sin to so much as enter a non-Catholic house of worship. What were they afraid of? Holding the threat of damnation over your head if you leave their faith was and is the only way to keep people "in line." Again, God is getting a bad rap. He is not insecure! So ask away! You might actually find the truly loving God that He is. As the First Commandment so presciently puts it, "You shall have no other gods before me." Put your faith in God, not your faith.

In tribal societies, nature (wind, water, fire, the earth, the air/sky, plants, creatures) is infused with the Divine Spirit. Early man had his own understanding of God, and other names for Him. Any violence against, exploitation of, and waste of nature was seen as a transgression against that Spirit. No one owned the land or anything on it. Imagine their shock and sadness at the aggression of these new people coming to the land and wantonly ripping it apart.

They saw men killing buffalo for sport from a moving train. The newcomers seemed to have had no regard for the animal and what it had to offer in the way of food and clothing and beauty. Would that be worth fighting a war over?

I wonder what our world would be like today had Native Americans won that war. Since power and greed are common among all mankind, no matter what their beliefs, the outcome might have been the same. Tribal societies fought amongst each other for control too, and some made slaves of their captives. So, we might have inherited a greener planet, but not necessarily a fair or peaceable one.

In many organized religions the repression of women is accepted. Most religions have their own story of creation. We're all familiar with the biblical story of creation, wherein Eve was made from Adam's rib to serve as his partner and, in her weakness, succumbed to the serpent's blandishments and tempted Adam to partake of the forbidden fruit. The "first original sin" – simple disobedience – is why, it is believed, we are born in sin. There is an assumed need to be forgiven for even having been born. Really? According to some religious traditions, even those with different creation myths, women must accept the role of passive and maternal presence – when she's not being a sexy temptress – seldom one of authority or independence. She might hold a place of honor or even be "put on a pedestal," but not one of power. There have been serious consequences to pay when she enlarged that role. Somehow it gets overlooked that if it weren't for this original sin and the desire to taste the Tree of the Knowledge of Good and Evil, there would possibly be no one but Adam and Eve on Earth. When they were cast from the Garden of Eden Cain was conceived, and life with the knowledge of good and evil begins. There is no recorded evidence of children before Cain. Why is that? In either case, it was eating the fruit that gave us the knowledge of good and evil allowing life with a choice and it was woman who gave birth. Maybe we should thank her. What do you think – a sin, or God's plan? Might the world be different and more peaceful if women had the dominant role, or would women be corrupted by power and wealth as well? I suppose this question can not fairly be answered, but who knows? Maybe that day will come.

It's no wonder people doubt the existence of God. The anthropomorphic concept of God that many of us have inherited has been used to control the people through government and religious doctrine. But He's also called upon as the greatest source of love and comfort. Wow, talk about opposites! We see a world of difference in the "divine knowledge" these religious leaders have of what God wants. It's the love and comfort you get from your beliefs that matter, not the bickering and fighting over who's right and who's wrong. That would be the opposite of what God wants. Can you see that?

The Catholic Church professes to be the first Christ-centered church to come into power. And as we have seen, it played an enormous role in the governing of several countries. A great deal of money and unquestioning allegiance from a sheep-like following were the payoffs. Those who followed a different belief system were simply burned at the stake, jailed, or shunned. Problem solved. You could become one of the sheep or face dire consequences. After all, there could be only one church. Sadly, with that power came massive corruption, and the splits from that one church began.

The Protestant Reformation began in 1517, when Luther posted his "Ninety-five Theses" on the door of the Castle of Wittenberg. Composed in Latin, Luther's many questions and objections to Church doctrine and devotional practices quickly made the rounds to archbishops and other superiors. The Protestant Reformation survived the resulting persecutions, opening the door to other Christian religions. The Roman Catholic Church was no longer the only Christian church.

For members of an intelligent species to kill one another over differences in the way they see and worship God is virtually unbelievable. Physics teaches that we are all one, and made of the same stuff the entire universe is made of. We are particles of energy. Is it not arrogant to vainly assume that your belief is better than the others, and to believe God needs you to fight His "battles?" Why do we need "soldiers of the cross?" It must be sad for our Father in Heaven to see His children fighting over how they show their love for Him. It makes no sense, and is very, very sad.

While it is open to a wide range of interpretation, many religions worldwide use the Bible as the basis for their beliefs, which accounts for the many varied religions. Ever try to count the number of different Christian religions alone? It's safe to say that there are many different ways of looking at any one particular religion. And there are different sects within many of the major religions. Surely everything would have been made clearer if it were important to God. Why does it matter so much to us, when it clearly doesn't matter to God?

Most Western religions have taught that upon death we will be judged, then sent directly to heaven – provided we subscribed to the "right" religious beliefs and lived a reasonably decent life – or punished for all eternity if we have not. The reward for our righteousness is to spend eternity with Him in Paradise. I believe that God, in his unspeakable immensity and beauty, would be far beyond the need to sit on a throne and pass judgment. Do you need a threat hanging over you to be a decent person? Like our judicial system that has not been able to stop, or put much of a dent in crime, the so-called "wrath" of God hasn't, either. The only thing that can change such misconceptions is to know that we are beloved and eternal beings, all of us. The choices we make today play the leading role in our eternal joy or temporary woe, and the present life we're living.

Not being baptized, being born gay, or committing suicide, I was taught, could land a person in hell. Many of them have lived their own hells here on Earth, or at least suffered hellish experiences, so why would He condemn them – or *any* of his creations – to hell for eternity? It makes no sense. Maybe the so called sinners among us are here to teach us to be nonjudgmental, tolerant, and forgiving. When a belief causes more damage than good, it really needs a second look. Imagine the grief it causes so many people to wonder if their loved one – say, their unbaptized baby – might be in hell. Is that the God you want to spend eternity with? "Religious" teaching that all nonbelievers (of *their* religion) are marked for eradication is absurd. How do such radical beliefs get started? Interpretation? Or is it power they want? A good person who didn't hear the word, are they in hell, as so many still believe? Why would God do that? Many religions believe hell exists, but would an all-loving God possibly send the children He loves to such a place? Hell sounds more like something man would create, not an all-loving God.

NDEers indicate that judgment may not be what we've been taught it is. Imagine you've just arrived in a heavenly realm and immediately you feel God's love. This all-consuming love is far greater than any love you have ever felt. It's total, and unconditional. Instantly, you're filled with the memories of your life on Earth and the joy and pain you brought to others. How can you bathe in God's love when you know, and can actually *feel*, the pain you caused His children? For now you know they are your family too! Religion teaches forgiveness. How long will you have to wait for that forgiveness to come, or more to the point, what will it take for you to forgive yourself? This could be hell, couldn't it? A torment more mental than physical. It's something to think about.

Some religions believe that after death, an astral or etheric body stays with you, or that you flit around in some other kind of spirit body, or are reunited with the physical body when Gabriel blows his horn to announce Judgment Day. If that's the case, you would probably feel physical pain. But if you believe as I do that we are energy, it should give you pause to wonder what kind of pain that body of energy would feel. I rather like the idea of not being confined to a physical body. Don't get me wrong. I've loved my body and it has served me well, but when the time comes to leave it, I'll be ready. It seems that man himself has ghostwritten the horrors of hell, and not God. If you are allowed to experience the pain and suffering you caused, the agonies of hell would have more to do with emotional pain than physical pain. Remember, when these ancient texts were being written, torture was the punishment for transgressions. If they were written today, I think they would be very different.

Beliefs surrounding birth control should also be looked at. Overpopulation of the planet is a very serious problem. How could birth control possibly be a sin? The Bible urges us to "go forth and multiply." It doesn't say it's a sin not to multiply. Are the people who can't reproduce living in sin? When the house is full and food is in short supply, it becomes selfish and irresponsible to continue to multiply. We are polluting our beautiful oceans, cutting down whole forests, and stripping our land of nutrients necessary for growing food that is nourishing. We need to take responsibility for this beautiful green planet He created for us, and keep it beautiful and healthy for centuries to come. This is a choice we clearly need to make.

Early Christians were told that the end was near, at which time their suffering would end. It was discouraging when that didn't happen. Over the centuries, conceptions of "the end" changed as the horrors of hell took center stage. Christians had no trouble accepting that "the wicked" would eventually suffer, and the believers resurrected, "raptured," and taken up to Heaven. Sweet revenge would finally be realized! I learned of the end times when I was a child. It was supposed to come like a thief in the night, but no one knew when. We were told the prophecies would be fulfilled, and that end times were coming soon. To a child, that's pretty scary. I was told there would be a rapture, in which God's people would be taken directly to heaven just before the end. The world would be a terrifying place after the end, and I was very afraid. Would I be taken and someone I love be left behind? Ah, but I needn't have worried! When asked whether the spectacle of their hell-tortured loved ones would sadden those in heaven, Luther replied, "Not in the least." That's just cold! The gates to heaven were narrow, I was taught, and those to hell very wide. You prayed you had dotted all your i's and crossed your t's and that everyone you loved had too. How sad and cruel it is that we terrify our children like that.

However, there may be another chance for yourself and the people you love. Purgatory and limbo were created as midway stations between heaven and hell. Before the concept was officially put to rest in 2007, limbo was hypothesized as a place where infants go who have not been baptized; while there would be no punishment there, babies (and in some cases, righteous pagans) would be eternally deprived of the joy of God's presence. In purgatory, one could contemplate his or her life, make amends for sins and, with God's mercy, ascend into heaven. You or your family could also pay the church for "indulgences" whereby priests intervene on your behalf when you die, to have your sins forgiven within a swifter and more expeditious timeframe. Most religions have similar stories concerning the afterlife. I don't know – it just all seems so manmade to me, and just another source of income and power for the church.

One wonders what might have been lost or even added in the many translations of the Bible. The Old Testament was translated from Hebrew, to Greek, to Latin, and then finally to English. The New Testament went from Greek, to Latin, and then English. Also, many of these texts were deleted, lost, and often destroyed. Just for the historical value alone, it would have been nice to have them.

The priest who first translated the Bible to English, William Tyndale [1495-1536], was accused of perverting the scriptures. He was strangled and burned at the stake. Later (to his reported relief in purgatory, where he was sent for harboring resentment), he was acquitted and given the title "Father of the English Bible." I guess that would be the consolation prize for all his hard work. No wonder people were afraid to question or speak against these sacralized texts, let alone try to translate them.

The King James Version came along in 1611. The Revised Standard Version was published in 1952, and the New Revised Version in 1989. In all, there are over 26 versions of the Bible and more than 200 Christian denominations. And that's just one religion. Viewed mainly as a history book by some and as a fascinating compilation of myths and legends by others, millions more take the Bible as the literal truth. I often wonder how a person 3000 years ago might have interpreted an airplane in the sky or even an earthquake. So for me, things just aren't so black-and-white.

Many religious Christians put their faith in the whole Bible, some in the Old Testament only, some in the New, and some in other texts. Those with more interest in science and facts tend to view it from an historical perspective. It's all good. If you find inspiration and peace in your beliefs and let everyone else find the same in their own beliefs, then guess what? There will be peace. Remember, God is not religion. He was here long before religion. Man created religion.

Love is at the core of most religions, affirming unity. The dogmas and interpretations that separate one religion from another cause separation. Sadly, somewhere along the line we missed the point. Whatever religion you choose to express your love for God and your fellow man is and should remain an individual matter. God's religion truly is LOVE, just love. Love is universal and unifying.

Jesus was a Hebrew teacher educated in the temples and authorized to speak from its platforms. He spoke of a loving and forgiving God and not an angry God to be feared. He spoke against some of the rituals of the time, such as the pilgrimage to Jerusalem to pay tithes. He caused a great deal of fear in religious leaders, and we all know how that turned out for him. He didn't teach Christianity because it didn't exist. He taught love, forgiveness, and the personal connection between you and a loving God. His teachings spread after His death and Christianity became a recognized religion some 300 years later. His teachings are recorded in the New Testament. It's clear to me that if we were to honor the teachings of love and forgiveness Jesus taught, there would be no need of the Ten Commandments Moses handed down. There would be no need for rules at all.

Hinduism is a collection of religious beliefs and practices that grew slowly over thousands of years, some say beginning among tribes as early as 5500-2600 B.C. There is no one founder connected to it. Hindus believe in many or one God, because He can be many or one, as He chooses. Buddhism developed outside of Hinduism. It does not support the caste system as Hinduism does, but like the Hindus, Buddhists believe in karma and reincarnation. There has never been a military crusade in the name of Buddha. It seems to be more a philosophy than a religion. Islam was established in the year 610, when Muhammad received the Qur'an from the angel Gabriel. Muslims believe it is the faith of Adam. The Jewish faith is believed to be the oldest of monotheistic (belief in one god) religions. Although, some scholars believe that Zoroastrionism is older than Judaism. That was interesting to me because I had never heard of that religion. But then again there are a lot of religions out there. The Ten Commandments and obedience to them are expected in Judaism. Judaism differs from Christianity in that it teaches that the savior who was predicted in the Old Testament to come and save us from sin, has not yet been born. After all, Jesus wasn't a king of wealth and power, which was how He was prophesied to be in scripture. Christians believe Jesus was that Savior, the Son of God who reigns as the King of Man, not the land. They further believe that all who accept Him as their Lord and Savior will enter the Kingdom of Heaven. I believe He only wanted us to understand and practice what He taught, and not necessarily believe in His person. He truly *is* the savior for all who can live what He taught. Interpretation, interpretation.

There are usually offshoots and various philosophies within each religion. Many people take their faith (which sometimes means what parents and loved ones have told them from an early age) to be the true and only way to God. How can so many religious people, believing theirs to be the only "right" religion, not at least consider the possibility of truth in other religions? Surely all religions got *something* right. After all, most started with a divine message or inspiration. So, relax! You got it right, and so does everyone else.

It's just possible we'll find God through science and not religion. It was science that proved the Earth was not the center of the universe. But not before scores of "heretics" were burned at the stake, tortured, or imprisoned for voicing their doubt. Thank God — science survived, and continues to solve mysteries today. One's religion cannot eradicate a proven truth. It's also understandable why science would be slow to recognize anything having to do with the God of religion.

Every day, science makes discoveries proving the oneness of everything by demonstrating the connection between all things. It is a world that is unseen; it's the quantum world. It's God's world. Without fear of persecution from religious factions, men and women of science have the freedom to look at all possibilities. It is only ridicule from other scientists that slow things down. But curiosity will always prevail and result in progress.

CHAPTER EIGHT

Raising a Spiritual Child

If I knew then what I know now, I would
have raised my daughter differently.

If I knew then, what I know now." How often do we say that? As I was researching, I began to realize how important it is to raise our children with the knowledge of their true origin. I believe my and Bre's lives would have been less stressful and more meaningful had I known this. I would have been a more conscious parent, open to the wonder of the spirit inside her. This would have validated who she was more than my response to the human child I saw. I can only imagine how different our lives would have been. Perhaps it's not too late for you to know, so I'm adding this chapter.

There are children being born today who are believed to be exceptionally evolved, the children of the future. Star Children or Indigo Children are familiar names for these young ones, although there are other names. There also seem to be a number of interpretations of just who, how, and why they are. Most are gifted with special or paranormal abilities, and are generally intuitive, highly sensitive, dazzlingly intelligent, and wise beyond their years. They are in touch with their true identity and their origin, where love was all they knew. If they're not taken seriously and nurtured, they put up walls to protect themselves, and all that sensitivity is buried. They can become very angry or disappointed with life when they're not validated and appreciated. It is important to recognize these talents and proclivities in the first five years of life, when everything they hear and feel is ingrained into their subconscious. Maybe you believe you have one of these children; if so, there are books on this subject.

Bre had an inner wisdom that surprised me sometimes for someone so young. She was very sensitive to people's feelings and had her "imaginary" friends. Things were black-and-white for her, and she couldn't understand why they weren't for others. I should have been seriously listening to all she had to impart, knowing there was an old and wise spirit inside her. Does that make her a star child? It's possible this phenomenon is not new, but is only recently being recognized and no longer hidden away due to our lack of understanding. Will this recognition open the door to mankind's next major evolution? I believe that people who are given free rein to express their compassion and intuitive awareness of the oneness of all things could create Heaven on Earth.

The Children of Now, by Meg Blackburn Losey, Msc.D., Ph.D., is a book about these special children. She theorizes that autism could come about from lack of recognition. To protect their sensitivities, kids with these "disorders" put up walls and withdraw into themselves. This opened a memory of a documentary I watched on a family with an autistic child who had given up on medical intervention. The family decided to mimic everything the child did. If he sat in a corner and stared at the wall, they did the same. If he ran around the room and flapped his arms, they did the same. Everyone living in the house or coming to the house was instructed to do likewise. They didn't resist; whatever he did was seen to be completely normal. In time, he began to open up and is now functioning as any healthy man. Did this child finally feel validated and begin to feel less afraid to let down his walls? If you have an autistic child you can research Son-Rise, a facility who's philosophy is based on these principles.

In Losey's book, a four-year-old boy is quoted as saying: "I remember what it was like to be home. It was a lot different than here. Everything was beautiful. I loved everyone and they loved me back. How come it doesn't feel like that here?"

The worst thing that could happen to me happened when I lost Bre. It put into perspective all the things I thought were so important. Suddenly, none of those things mattered and nothing made sense to me anymore. That's what my beautiful daughter taught me. Love is all there is. None of that small stuff mattered.

Most of us like stuff, and accumulating more stuff. It gives us pleasure to see and use and display our stuff. The home, the car, the jewelry, the shoes (I love shoes) — lots of stuff. Walking into my daughter's home that day, I saw all her stuff. She loved her stuff. She took pride in rescuing old stuff off a junk pile and making it come to life. I loved that about her. She just couldn't understand why people didn't recycle more than paper and cans. But, there it was, still here, and she was not. Strange as it sounds, I wanted her to have it with her; it belonged to her and it should be with her, not here. Stuff lost all meaning to me that day. Stuff is fine to have, even to take pleasure in, but it's not who you are. Who you are is what you take with you when you leave the stuff behind.

Bre left at great sacrifice to herself, so what purpose could it serve? She didn't want to leave her husband, me, her many friends and family, and most especially, her son. She was an unselfish, caring person, who always had your back. She believed in justice and consequence. It was right or it was wrong. If you borrowed money, she made sure you paid it back, even if you owed it to someone else. It was the right thing to do. She couldn't understand why anyone would sit back and let things happen to them. If it was wrong, it needed to be made right. If there was a misunderstanding, she would be on the phone or at your house until you talked it through. Old boyfriends remained friends. Like she said, "We were friends once, and that shouldn't change just because it didn't work out." It didn't seem to make sense to her any other way. She was completely loyal to her friends and family. My nephew's new wife told me that of all Aaron's family, she was most nervous about meeting Bre. She'd been briefed on how protective Bre was, and knew she'd be asked a lot of questions. I had to laugh, because it was true. She wasn't afraid to ask the questions and to my surprise, people would answer. I think that's because she had a caring innocence about her questions and not idle curiosity.

I always felt Bre was a gift; she saved my life and gave it meaning. I don't think she really understood just how wonderful I thought she was. Because, guess what – I didn't tell her. I just assumed she knew. Don't make that mistake. Your children need to know what a gift they are to you and how lucky you are they chose you as their parents in this life. It would add value and joy to their life. Then watch your child grow. How often do parents say or feel, "I gave you life, raised and nurtured you. Sacrificed for you. You owe me." The truth could be the other way around. They came because of you, and could be teaching you.

In *The Seat of the Soul*, author Gary Zukav reminds us: "Love does not seek to control, but to nurture; it does not dominate, but empowers." Too many people in close relationships, such as parent-child and husband-wife, seem to believe that under the wise, protective umbrella of their control, everyone is safe and all is well. But far from it! Such lives are frustrating to both controller and controlee, as one life is narrowed to the scope of the controller, while the other is diminished by anger and fear. Really, it's insecurities and fear that fuel the need to control. And it's so sad to witness. What children learn from that is fear and worry. We need to let go of the preconceived ideas about what we think their life, as well as our own, should be like. Teach them to go with the flow of life without fear. Life is an adventure, a journey full of possibilities, and a very short one. We take away from their individuality, as well as their voice, when we expect them to conform to our way of thinking or what we think society expects. They're here for the same reasons we're here – to learn. Our children are much smarter than we think, and maybe we're not quite as smart as we think. Let them say what they have to say with no fear of ridicule or reprimand. It's not always backtalk. You'll be amazed at their inner knowledge. We are never too old to learn something, even from our children.

John Lennon had the right view of life when he said, "Life is what happens to you while you're busy making other plans." He understood that we don't have control over life. Life has a way of taking us where it wants to go. So, plan your life, but be prepared to go with the flow. There is always a big, cooperative picture playing. If it doesn't seem to be working out the way you think it should, remember this story from Dan Millman's book, *Wisdom of the Peaceful Warrior*:

Good Luck, Bad Luck

An old man and his son worked a small farm, with only one horse to pull the plow.

One day, the horse ran away.

"How terrible," sympathized the neighbors. "What bad luck."

"Who knows whether it's bad luck or good luck," the farmer replied.

A week later, the horse returned from the mountains, leading five wild mares into the barn.

"What wonderful luck!" said the neighbors.

"Good luck? Bad luck? Who knows?" answered the old man.

The next day, the son, trying to tame one of the horses, fell and broke his leg.

"How terrible. What bad luck!"

"Bad luck? Good luck?"

The army came to all the farms to take the young men to war, but the farmer's son was of no use to them, so he was spared.

"Good? Bad?"

This farmer understood the idea of acceptance and appreciation. Acceptance is always the first action to take. Not complacency – acceptance. There's a big difference. Life happens with or without it. Acceptance removes the stress and worry, knowing nothing stays the same. Let's teach our children that. Things can't change while we're in a state of resistance. "The more you resist, the more it persists." Nothing can deprive us more of what we want than the thought we give to what we don't have, so go with the flow. There is wisdom to be gained in that flow.

What would happen if our children knew they were eternal beings and on a wonderful journey of exploration and growth? Can we even accept that for ourselves? I think they would develop a deeper appreciation for the gift of life and live it more freely, with less fear and stress. Instead, we focus most of our attention on crossing t's, dotting i's, and fitting in to society's expectations. Although some of this focus may have value, it's not as important as we think. There is a wonderfully liberating school for children called Waldorf. It goes beyond basics and incorporates the spiritual and empathetic aspects, also stressing the role of the imagination in learning across all disciplines. If I had small children I would look into the philosophies of Waldorf School, founder Rudolf Steiner, so I'm including this information for you if you're interested.

Teach your child that there is a lesson in all situations, wherein lies the opportunity to learn and experience whatever life may bring. Nothing stays the same. There is an ebb and flow to life, sometimes looking and seeming bad, and sometimes looking and seeming good. It keeps changing, and you change with it. It's easy to put yourself in a place of self-pity and doubt during the bad times. But if you allow the flow to happen, knowing there is a bigger picture playing, you'll be more accepting until you can see (or at least glimpse) it yourself. This is something I found very hard to do when I lost Bre. Even though my view of life has changed dramatically, there will never be a reason good enough for her not to be here. I now accept that and know she'll explain it to me when I see her again.

Helen Keller, blind and deaf from birth said, "When one door of happiness closes, another opens. We look so long at the closed door we do not see the one that has opened for us". Although I can't say I've opened a happy door, many other doors have opened. And it will for you and your children as well. Don't get stuck at the closed door.

Remember, everyone is important and on their own journey. It may sometimes be hard to imagine your child as having a personal journey, but that's exactly why he or she is here. Your only responsibility is to love and to guide. It's easy to be bossy when you assume the position of "older and wiser." I hope I was never bossy. I'm just sorry I didn't look into Breana's inner wisdom more, instead of seeing her as a child.

As parents, we are supposed to teach and model right from wrong, giving love and wisdom as we know it. The knowledge we have was passed down to us by our parents and peers, and collected through our experiences. But does that make it true? That knowledge should offer encouragement and a good, uplifting feeling that accompanies it. If it doesn't, it's not true. Evaluate what you've been taught; don't just go on autopilot. If holding on to old beliefs brings you joy, then hold on to them, but if not, they're NOT true, so let them go.

This planet and our very existence are miracles. Let's teach our children that we are responsible for the health of this beautiful place we call Earth and to have respect for all living things, as they are miracles as well. Instinctively they are aware of this, and their spirits will sigh with relief when you remind them. If you don't, walls go up and it's buried. Litter and waste won't be any big deal for them, if it isn't for you.

A child's imagination is a beautiful and fascinating thing. Is the world they just came from a place where anything you can imagine is possible? NDE indicates that that is the reality there. Is their wonderful imagination a residue of that state? We didn't teach them to imagine, so where did they learn it? Sadly, we soon teach them that it's a fun play thing, but not real. What would happen if we explored what they know, giving it validation, rather than what *we* know? Having an active imagination is a very good thing. It would surely be fun and informative to explore their wonderful imaginations. Play along and imagine with them!

I often wonder when a mother can't seem to put her baby down, if she is starving for the love oozing from her baby. That love is hard to resist for many of us. A child comes into this world completely trusting, nonjudgmental, full of love and wonder. The world they've just left was void of all fear, leaving only love, which would explain the trust they are born with. At birth they enter the negative environment of earth and walls begin to go up when love isn't felt. By the time they are three they've forgotten that world and are now living in this world, which in our fear for their wellbeing teaches them there is a lot to fear. I'm not saying let them play in the street, but there is a balance in how we guide them. Here's an example: "John get out of the street! You can get hit by a car and hurt very badly!" or "John get out of the street! Streets are for cars. If a car hit and hurt you it would be very sad for the driver, for you, and for me." Although both show concern, one teaches fear and the other consideration.

Oprah had a show inviting parents with large families to share their ideas on why their children grew up to be successful adults. One man said, "I never told my children no. I only told them of the possible consequences of each choice they make." This father's whole philosophy had to do with choice. That struck me as a good way to teach children how to make conscious decisions as adults. This program was also where I picked up the idea of giving children an old checkbook to track their money in. Money is something to respect and use wisely, not love and spend unconsciously.

It seems so much of life is about making choices, and there's no school for making the right choice every time. But here are a few things that may help. A choice will often have a good or bad feeling attached to it. That feeling is not the same thing as "Let your conscience be your guide." Your conscience has a lot of self-talk in it, but you can trust your raw and unedited feelings, because I believe God gave us the capacity to feel to serve as our guidance system. When your mind says "Do this," you may believe it's right, but does it feel good? Are you at peace? If not, think it through again. Much of our consciousness is shaped and led by religion, teachers, parents, and peers – and not God. Always ask yourself: *How does this make me feel?* I think we sometimes are confused between our conditioning and that good feeling that comes from the heart.

Are you envious, jealous, or critical of others and what they have? Or are you truly happy for them and what they appear to have? How does each of these states feel? Which feeling feels good? You can choose to be envious, suspicious, and ill-willed, which doesn't feel good, or you can choose to feel kind and happy. When you judge someone for their lifestyle, beliefs, or even how they look, how does that feel?

Do you feel joy, or do you feel righteous and powerful? You'll be happier if you let God be the judge. Your life and everyone around you will be happier if you remember to choose the good feeling.

Whenever we make choices, there is fear of possible negative consequences. Wisdom is gained when we learn from those consequences. As wisdom grows, the choices we make become increasingly wise. I believe that's why we are here. Fear stops us from making choices and stunts our growth. Ask yourself, *What am I afraid of?* or *What's the worst thing that could happen and how would I deal with that?* Now make the choice, because "the only wrong choice is no choice at all." It's important that our children know **they will survive the choices** they make, and go on to make more choices with the wisdom they gain throughout their life.

Did you know there is a negative vibration that accompanies every lie? If you have ever told a lie you may have experienced that feeling; and telling a lie that hurts someone else is the most damaging lie. In excess, that negative vibration can cause pain and disease in the body. We teach our children to lie when we punish them for telling the truth. Breana knew she would not be in trouble for telling the truth. In fact, I thanked her. However if she lied and I found out about it, she would not only be in trouble, it would diminish the trust we have. Relationships start with trust and it is important that our children have that understanding.

Self-esteem should be at the top of your wish-list for your child. When our children look to us for approval and validation, we generally tell them how proud we are of them, but more important is the need to tell them how proud they should be of themselves. Being proud of yourself is liking yourself, and liking yourself means growing into an adult who no longer looks for approval from others for self-validation. Self-liker's become leaders, not followers who do everything they're told to do. They have the confidence to think things through for themselves. An interesting question to ask your child is, "Do you like who you are?" Don't be surprised if they look stunned by that question, and be prepared to tell them why you like who they are. Perhaps they are caring, compassionate, truthful, not critical of others, a good listener, smart, able to resist peer pressure, etc. You'll have fun and so will they. Children are inclined to become what you teach them to become.

It's impossible to be a good parent if you don't appreciate who you are and who others are. Ask yourself the same question, "Do you like who you are?" It feels strange, doesn't it? Love yourself, just as God does. Forgive yourself, just as God does. You have great value and so does everyone else. Being critical of yourself because you don't know your value is the most destructive thing you can do, so don't do it. It's simply not true. It doesn't feel good, does it? Remember God's guiding system, always ON inside of you. It tells you when it feels good and when it feels bad. One is true, one is not. Remember that? That is God's gift to you.

In *The Mind of Your Newborn Baby*, David Chamberlain says: "The truth is, much of what we have traditionally believed about babies is false. They are not simple beings, but complex and ageless – small creatures with unexpectedly large thoughts."

Babies process much more information than we once believed. In fact, EEG studies show that a child under the age of six is usually functioning in the alpha mode similar to hypno-sis. It's how they learn so quickly, but it's also why what they learn is so deeply ingrained into their subconscious. The subconscious cannot tell the difference between what is true and what is not. When we're older, we can analyze things using our conscious mind, which tells our subconscious what is or isn't true and how we feel about what we've been told or experienced. Babies are very aware but don't yet have this ability so all that is presented to them becomes an accepted fact. The subconscious is working on autopilot, telling them they are smart or dumb, deserve the best or the worst, that they have value or no value, etc. No matter what the con-scious mind says, it is filtered through the subconscious. Fill their subconscious with awareness of self-worth, because it's very hard to find independently, as adults. It's never too late to make a difference in your child's life or in your own, so start now.

Teach your child to live in the moment. We have all heard and read about that, but if it isn't taught to us and modeled by adults in our childhood, it's hard to make it our way in adult life. When they brush their teeth, we might suggest to our children that they pay attention to each tooth, why they do it, and how the brush feels against their gums. Point out the butterfly, its beautiful wings, how it moves and sucks nectar from the beautiful flowers. Join them in looking up at the imagination-sparking forms in the clouds. My grandson and I love to look out at the water and imagine all the sea life swimming in it. Where are they going and what are they doing? Ask: *What do you see, hear, smell, feel, taste?* Whatever, just pay attention to the moment. Appreciate the moment. Don't think about the last moment or the next moment. It's either happened or it hasn't happened yet. Every moment is now, and it's all you have. Listen to people as though it's the most important moment — and utterance — of all time. How often do you let your mind wander and miss the moment? I'm not sure who coined the saying, "The beauty of each moment becomes the beauty of your life," but it is so true.

I missed so many moments with my own daughter and now those moments are gone. Don't miss those incredible moments.

CHAPTER NINE

Near–Death Experience (NDE)

The people who have had this
experience know with absolute
certainty that we do not die.

We know so little about death. We simply stop. Our heart stops, our breathing stops, our brainwaves stop. We simply cease to exist. But, is that really true?

I think one of the reasons we know so little about death is that we're afraid of death. It's easier to say when we die, *Well, that's it.* No judgment, no nothing. Just sleep, peaceful sleep. For many, to look any further borders on the paranormal or religious territories. Some believe that to consider any possibilities beyond nothingness is foolish. And let's face it: many ideas about the afterlife are pretty far-fetched. There is creditable and credible research into whether the consciousness survives, however. Which of course is really asking, *Is there life after death?*

For anyone who has had a near-death experience (NDE), there is no question. It is absolutely true. They were in a very real place, where they felt an all-consuming love and acceptance. Many were met by friends and family who had passed before them. Most of us have heard or read about this, but most of us haven't experienced it. So we're left with a lot of skepticism, waiting for science to explain it. Yet the people who have experienced it are convinced it was real – realer than real, in fact – and no amount of discussion or scientific knowledge can convince them otherwise. That's interesting, don't you think?

Some believe that when the body dies, so too does the consciousness. We are made of matter, yet there is an energy flow within us. What happens to all that energy? If Einstein had it right, "Energy can be neither created nor destroyed; it can only be changed from one form to another." So where is it? That is the question, isn't it? Is that energy our consciousness and who we truly are? Through my search for Bre and all the paths it led me down, my strong belief has become that energy, soul, and consciousness are the very same thing.

Most NDEs happen when the heart stops and the neocortex of the brain is temporarily inactive. Because there is still some activity in the brain, science has explained it as a primitive brain-stem program, an hallucination brought on by an anesthetic, or just the wild dream of a dying brain. That may explain some, but not all.

In his bestselling book *Proof of Heaven*, Harvard neurosurgeon Eben Alexander describes his NDE and the journey he took on the Other Side. The neocortex of his brain was not just inactive but nonexistent, reduced by bacterial meningitis to "mush." His out-of-body experience left Dr. Alexander with absolute certainty that the experience he had was real. The neocortex of his brain was not functioning, yet there he was, experiencing this incredible journey. After a period in "lower" realms, he was guided upward by a beautiful person who filled his mind with incredible amounts of scientific knowledge. He didn't recognize her, and later wondered why. The patients who subsequently spoke of their NDEs with him had said they knew the people who met them. As it turned out, the beautiful woman was a biological sister whom Eben, an adoptee, had never met and only learned about when shown a picture of her months later. I hope he doesn't mind my giving you that bit of information, because there is a lot more to his amazing journey. As a scientist, he hadn't believed in NDE before his own experience. Now, he wanted to give validation to the patients he hadn't believed. There no explanation for it, only that it was very real. Real enough that he was eager to tell his story to others. He wasn't worried about the criticism that might follow, only the importance of what he had to say.

The experiences of NDE'ers have a lot of similarities, but some differences too. There are varying amounts of time that a person spends in an NDE, from seconds to days. The longer they are there, the more information they are given.

It is said to be a wholly peaceful place, with a feeling of being loved far beyond anything they have ever experienced on Earth. They feel complete acceptance and a connection with all things, a sense of oneness and beauty they can't explain. There are colors they've never seen, and beautiful music that permeates their whole being is felt, as well as heard. It's as though everything is truly alive.

For many, there is a life review of sorts where you see and feel the effects your actions had on others during your life, both good and bad. Although it is painful at times, it is said to feel more like a learning experience than a judgment. The experiencer's life is changed as a result of the NDE, and the changes are beneficent and permanent. No wonder they are so certain!

Space and time have no reality there. Some say they are illusions, created to serve as coordinates for our physical life. You seem to be everywhere and in every time, all at the same time, and the only time is now. Such a state exceeds our grasp, yet those who are there seem to completely understand it. Einstein would love it and so would quantum physicists.

The mystery of this dimension seems to coincide with the mystery of quantum mechanics. States like non-locality, where you are everywhere at once, can be very hard to explain with the vocabulary we have. Once connected, always connected, seems to be the reality there. The invisible world of quantum mechanics sounds a lot like the world we live in after death. Just something to think about and something I've thought about a lot.

Some are shown the Big Bang, and many Big Bangs, creating endless universes, as well as given a sense of how they are a part of that living system. Is that living system God? This kind of mind-blowing information is hard to put words to, yet all that is imparted makes perfect sense to them as it unfolds.

Some pass through a tunnel or walk down a path toward an irresistibly loving light. A light so bright it would hurt the human eye. Then again, the eye is organic, and it appears we are energy, something quite different than organic matter. There is a sense of floating or flying, even if they are walking. Many are met by friends and family in joyous reunion, while others are met by a guide who takes them on a tour of this amazing place. Even pets have been there to greet them.

Information is instantaneously absorbed into their brain. Which makes sense, since the brain is matter, and deteriorates with death whereas consciousness is energy, and immortal. In an NDE, for any question that comes to mind, the answer is immediately there. This includes the greatest of profundities, such as how it all began and why we're here. It's not surprising that no one can explain it in simple terms when they come back. They do, however, know that all is as it should be. There is nothing to fear, life is eternal, and love is all there is. I think it is most telling that returnees no longer fear death. The good and bad experiences of life don't hold power over them as they did before their NDE. Life is just that – an experience.

NDEs don't seem to diminish traditional belief systems; they enhance them. A religious person may see and speak with figures from their own religious tradition; a scientist who didn't believe in God is infused with great volumes of scientific knowledge. But then again, God is the ultimate scientist. It seems all become more spiritual. God, the divine intelligence, or however you are comfortable explaining Him, becomes a certainty to them.

There is a shift in values, wherein love is more important than any material possession or personal achievement and status. The drive for riches and fame loses importance, for there is a far greater reason for their existence. They gain a reverence for all living things, living life more consciously, with acceptance and appreciation. I'm not saying that those who have had this experience give away all their worldly possessions; they simply appreciate all facets of life more fully and have a humbleness about it.

An NDE may also stimulate intuitive and psychic perception, as it did for my friend after his return. He was able to see and hear his parents, who assured him they were happy. It makes you wonder what our minds are capable of. If we had more understanding and less fear of death, I believe we would have more answers today. The research into death would be less restrictive if we knew we didn't die, but just passed to another plane. A plane that has always been there.

Having seen and felt the connection between all things, the ego of the experiencer (self-importance) takes a backseat, while their sense of true self-worth increases and all judgments fall away. They understand that everyone is on their own journey to discovery, which is equal in value to their own.

To me, some of the most interesting cases are when blind people (blind from birth) see for the first time. Although they can't describe a color specifically, they can describe the beauty of the things they saw. It seems too that perfect health is restored to everyone entering this dimension, but then again, we don't take our physical body with us. The spirit is, and always has been, perfect.

I can't leave this chapter without talking about the negative experiences some people have. They are rare, but it does happen to some. They think they've been to hell. I don't personally believe in hell, at least not in the biblical sense. I do, however, believe in negative energy created (of necessity) to accompany a life of contrasts. Without it, there would be no choices to make. It has to exist. Yet even those who have suffered an NDE "hell" report that their lives have subsequently changed – dramatically for the better – in much the same way as for people who had positive experiences. Some pass through this primordial dark space before they can see the light and are lifted out of that darkness, while others never get past it. It's a dark and scary place where the residents and/or phenomena have an ugliness about them. Are they repulsed by the beauty and love of the light, and choosing to stay in this place instead? If God's love is unconditional, then it makes sense that it is their choice. I wonder if this is why small children are afraid of the dark. Do they have a deep memory of this dark place?

There isn't much information about it because not many people actually experience it for any length of time, but it's definitely a place they don't want to return to. It is important to note its existence, if for no other reason than people have experienced it.

For some, the fact we are eternal and never die is unbelievable. Consequently, much doubt is cast upon the vast amounts of data collected and is also why so many choose not to look any further. Think of the leaps science could make if this incredible phenomena were accepted and studied. Many books have been written on the subject of NDE. Having experienced and then researched it, these authors are brave enough to write about it. They are very much appreciated.

In my search for Bre and where she might be, I read all I could find. It is through these many documented cases and the similarities in the quantum world that I began to realize it is a very real place. I believe this is where she is. I wish I could have an NDE and know with absolute certainty, as the people who have experienced it do, but I believe that the numerous and very credible accounts of these experiences are true. She is safe, she is loved, and I will see her again. Most importantly, I will understand why.

CHAPTER TEN

Reincarnation and Hypnosis

Eternity is a very long time,
so is it possible we choose to come
back again and again?

Reincarnation was an accepted part of Christianity from its inception. Some people interpret Jesus' words concerning Elijah in Matthew: 17 to mean that he had come back as John the Baptist. This could mean that Jesus believed in the recycling of life. But belief in reincarnation was opposed, and ultimately declared heretical, in the fourth century at the Council of Nicaea (the committee assigned the task by Roman Emperor Constantine of creating one Christian belief system, since there were many at the time). Reincarnation reappeared in the eleventh century in a Christian sect known as the Cathars, until the "one" church led a crusade to eliminate them. Of course, some religions and systems of philosophy have always embraced reincarnation as part of their belief system.

Because *this* is the life we are currently experiencing and not a former one, the truth or falsehood of physical rebirth shouldn't really matter and is probably why we don't remember past lives. The wisdom gained and/or trauma in those lives is all we could possibly bring with us to the next life. Still, it is a curiosity, and the investigation continues.

If the purpose of life is to teach, learn, or just experience life, then it does seem likely that we would decide to return. How could you experience everything in one short lifetime? What if you were born into an environment of fear and crime, where abuse was common, or into a sect or society offering only a life of prostitution, for example? How would these lives encourage growth or even much choice? While there is always some choice as to how one will respond to choicelessness – which could be a huge lesson in itself – many other opportunities for growth would be absent. In any case, each experience offers a wealth of lessons.

Some also believe that they will come back when they can be of service to the people they left. Oftentimes it will be as a sibling, a friend, or another family member. I know this sounds weird to some, but I used to feel Bre around me. I almost felt she could hear me, and left signs around for me to find. Signs like a note she had written me, or a picture I thought was lost or that someone gave me. If you have lost someone, you may know what I mean. When her son's little sister was born, I lost that feeling, along with the little signs. I wondered why and felt abandoned until I read about this phenomenon. I know she didn't want to leave her son, so I can understand her need to come back, especially in close association as his sister. I don't know. Coincidence?

If you think this may have happened in your life, remember that this little person is their own person. They generally have no memory of that other life. They have a new purpose and a new life. This life is the only life that is important now. It would be unusual for someone to come back so soon, as most will skip a few generations before returning. There is a need to heal – especially if the life had been traumatizing – and gather strength before coming back. And most lives usually are, in many ways, difficult. Basking in the love and acceptance they feel on the Other Side gives them the strength needed to return, if they choose.

It's also possible that my daughter felt a little space was needed for the healing process to continue in me. When you lose the most important person in your life, healing can move slowly. In either case, it is important to recognize that all things are the result of love. Whatever journey you are on, it has value, and will continue until the goal is reached, whether in this lifetime or in the next.

Another compelling case for reincarnation are the child prodigies who are born with intellect or talents far beyond the norm. By the time they are old enough to physically express it, astonishing ability in the arts, sciences, and/or music is apparent to their parents or caretakers. Others somehow hang on to dramatic memories: there is a child who remembers being a pilot in WWII, knows what his name was back then, and the name of his plane – even where he was shot down. Also, a mother who remembers her previous family, with memories that only the mother would hold – along with validation from her now elderly sons. There are many stories like this that can or have been authenticated. How can they be explained if the recycling of life isn't a possibility? Some say these memories are stored in our genes and passed down to future generations. That might account for some cases, but you would have to be related in order for memories to pass through genes, and many are not. Science offers no answers to these mysteries. Perhaps the recycling of life is the only answer.

Only fairly recently has it been discovered that hypnosis has value in psychiatry for opening closed doors, not only in this life, but in past lives as well. Talk therapy and drugs are the general treatments for patients suffering from various mental ills. However, when that doesn't work, some psychiatrists and psychologists will try hypnosis to uncover deep memories. It is during these times that a door to a past life can be intentionally or accidentally opened. Some doctors might feel inclined to close that door, while others sense a need to open it. Is it possible there is something in a past-life memory responsible for the patient's anguish? Whether the doctor believes in it or not, some are willing to use this approach when it may help the patient.

One such psychologist is Dr. Allan Botkin. His book is titled *Induced After-Death Communication*. He worked with veterans in healing grief and trauma. Talk therapy was not helping one of his patients, so he decided to try a form of hypnosis. (There are different methods of induction for hypnosis targeted to different parts of the brain.) Under hypnosis, the veteran had a visitation from a child he had watched die. The child, surrounded by brilliant light, smiled at him and thanked him for taking such good care of her. She wanted him to know how happy she was and that she loved him. From that moment on, the veteran began to heal.

The doctor wanted to write it off as an hallucination, but it was very real to the veteran, and the healing result was instantaneous. With patient consent, he began to use this form of hypnosis on others who did not respond to talk therapy. The results were the same. The possibility that these veterans were actually experiencing contact began to become a reality. Whether he believed it or not, this doctor decided that because it helps patients, it should be looked at more closely. His book was written in an effort to encourage research into this phenomenon.

This doctor was not interested in past-life regression, only in healing his patients with trauma in this life. This is true of other doctors trying to heal patients of unexplained fears, and are then surprised to find themselves in a past life situation. When it doesn't fall into the category of an hallucination, as many of these cases didn't, then what was it?

Dr. Brian Weiss, whose seminal book *Many Lives, Many Masters* broke major ground in the use of past-life hypnotic regression, was able to stop patients between lives, talking to them in this spiritual state. Their demeanor and intellect seemed to change in this environment, and the information revealed by these individuals was fascinating. It was the first time I had thought about the fact that we are truly two discrete beings, one human and one spirit, completely merged as one. You've heard it since you were young: "Listen to your conscience," "Follow your spirit," the soul within. I just never understood it as two beings in one. In fact, it sounds like science fiction to me. But then again, what about this book *doesn't* sound science fiction? Even science sounds like science fiction in the quantum world.

A friend told me she thinks of her body as a car. You're pretty attached to that car. You polish it and give it tune-ups, but eventually the motor stops and you need to leave that car. It served you well while you had it. It took you places you didn't want to go to and places you loved. You'll keep those memories and, if you choose, get a new car. In time, you'll forget that old car and collect memories in the new car. I myself plan to enjoy staying home for a very long time before I even look at a new car.

CHAPTER ELEVEN

Prayer

Does the quantum world hold
the blueprint to what prayer is?

Does prayer have a place in science? If all thoughts are energy and all thoughts can become reality, then are all thoughts just swirling around out there waiting to become reality? Is prayer a thought the universe or God receives? Is having "the faith of a little child" all that is needed to answer that prayer? Maybe it really is that simple.

The Bible says He knows our thoughts. But how could He, when there are billions of us? Are we truly a part of Him, and He a part of us? Most religions define God as being nonlocal. He is everywhere and in everything. When you pray, it doesn't go out there somewhere, but everywhere all at once. It is energy and energy is invisible. Just as gravity or electromagnetism can't be seen, so too are our thoughts and prayers. The difference is that prayer and thoughts do not weaken with distance as gravity and electromagnetism do. It seems you can pray for someone across the country or across the globe with the same effect as if you were standing next to them. The quantum world demonstrates that everything is connected, regardless of distance. The quantum world has so many similarities to the spiritual world that it has to at least give you pause.

In the invisible quantum reality, a person's thought waves cause changes to the behavior of particles. I wonder, is the Bible a blueprint of this world of quanta, wherein every thought can become reality, if you only believe? Did God create a universe that answers prayer, or does God answer prayer? Could both be the same? It's important to realize that God is not human in the sense that we think of as human.

There are ever so many books available on the power of positive thinking, such as *The Secret* by Rhonda Byrne, *Mind into Matter* by Fred Alan Wolf, *The Astonishing Power of Emotions* by Esther and Jerry Hicks, and *Ask and It Is Given*, also by Esther and Jerry Hicks, to name a few. It's interesting to compare the description of prayer in the Bible to what is written in these books – which is basically different versions of the power of thought. When you understand these ideas, and acknowledge God's love for you, you have the recipe for a more fulfilling life. You are not alone.

God said, "Let there be light," and it was so. The universe He created knew exactly what to do, and He knew exactly what to feel and intend to make it take the form of His thought. It seems that in order for matter to exist, the quantum world had to be created first. It's not magic, as I was more or less taught, but science. We are at the tip of discovery in this invisible world. Five hundred years from now, what will we have learned, and what powers unharnessed?

A thought always has feelings attached to it. Disbelief, anger, jealousy, envy, etc. and at the other end of the spectrum, compassion, love, forgiveness, gratitude, and a trust that all is well, are typical human feelings. And just as rocket fuel propels a rocket, it's the *feeling* behind the thought that drives the prayer. A prayer with a selfish or negative feeling behind it can only bring negative results. Even seemingly neutral feelings, like boredom and indifference, bring like results such as listlessness, lack of movement, and being "stuck" in the same-old-same-old. This is how the universe works; it can't do anything else. It was designed to give you your heart's desires. So ask yourself what's really in your heart when you pray. Try simply feeling grateful and saying thank you for the experience of life. Look for things to appreciate and stop dwelling on the things that you don't. One is positive, one is not. If you can be honest with yourself as to just what's going on in your head and your heart, your world just might change. In fact, I'm sure it will.

Most of us assume that Jesus was different from us. Yet that's not what He taught. He taught that the power is in each of us. "Whoever believes in me will also do the works that I do, and greater works than these will he do." (John 14:12) He also said, "I and my Father are one" (John 10:30) and "My Father is greater than I." (John 14:28) Is He trying to teach us that if you believe in what I am *saying* you can do these works, and yet in all things the Father knows best? Some may argue that I took this scripture out of context, but it's possible that a lot of the things He taught are taken out of context. It's the faith and love behind them that made these pronouncements stand out. Did He perform miracles, or did He just know God, the universe He created, and how it all worked?

I believe prayer has far more power than we know. A scientist might say our thoughts have far more power than we know. In any case, we aren't sure how to use that power – yet. The universe was created by design to work a certain way. It seems impossible to think it was an accident, or string of lucky coincidences.

In my reading, I came across an experiment in prayer called Spindrift. Plants were used to determine the type of prayer that had the most effect. You can read more about it in *Recovering the Soul*, by Larry Dossey, M.D. In one experiment they used rye seeds, praying for one set and not the other. Consistently, the ones prayed for would yield more than the ones not prayed for. The result was even more dramatic after one group of seeds was stressed with salt water. They discovered that the more prayer was given to the salt-watered seeds, and the more experienced the practitioner, the better the yield. An experienced practitioner would know exactly what to say and how to feel about it while praying.

It was also discovered that having the attitude of "Thy will be done," as opposed to holding a specific goal for the outcome, was more effective. We don't always know what the best outcome would be. I will always struggle with that, as I see no good reason for Bre to be gone. I do accept, however, that there is a bigger picture and that in reality, we do not die. Watching her son grow up without knowing her and the love she felt for him is a painful struggle for me every day. Every child deserves to feel that kind of love, but sadly, it's not always possible. Seeing her again is the only thing that will truly heal my heart and finally reveal to me the big picture.

When sad, stressful things happen in our life, we tend to tell God what we want. What we don't consider is the possibility that what we want is not always what should happen in order for our own and/or someone else's journey to continue in the best way possible. Wherever that journey takes you and the people you love, is the journey that your and their soul requires. All I can say is to keep praying for life to unfold as it should for the people you love and for yourself, with the least pain, best results, and the shortest route home. The hard part is to "let go and let God."

There's a group of little books written by Squire Rushnell titled, *When God Winks*. Very marked (freaky!) coincidences in our life, also known as synchronicities, may very well be the answer to spoken and unspoken prayer. Pay attention to those coincidences. I believe they could be more than weird stuff happening. They are easy to read and make you think about coincidences differently.

One NDE person told Bre's father that *she knew all things are as they should be, and all things are done in love. Whether it looks and feels good or bad, it has a purpose.* When we resist the bad stuff, oftentimes it gets worse. On the other hand, if we can figure out what the bad stuff is trying to tell us, we have a chance to reverse the path we're on and take a shorter, less painful route. We're here to learn, and whether we take the short route or the long route, we'll get there. At peace with whatever happened on Earth, this woman stressed that *heaven isn't what we think it is.* The love and acceptance she felt was immeasurable. I might add that this person gave the message to him years before we lost Bre. And it was this information that Bre's father gave me when I was at my lowest. Strange, isn't it, that this information was given to him years before and was passed on to me when I needed it most. Strange also that he picked up the phone at that moment to call me. Stranger still is the fact that this is the kind of information he would not have given any credence to under normal circumstances, yet it was exactly what I needed to hear.

If our thoughts are energy and we have the ability to project them into the universe, can we create order and harmony by simply concentrating? This is unimaginable power. When Jesus said, in Matthew 18:20, "For where two or three are gathered in my name, I am there among them," was He saying that a group concentrating on one thought has more power than one person alone? The shift in the electromagnetic field around Earth during 9/11 demonstrates that something BIG does happen when a large group is thinking the same thought. Maybe the day will come when everyone joins together in thoughts and feelings of peace. We are far from ready for it now, but we are evolving. Just something to think about and work toward.

CHAPTER TWELVE

Biology and Environment

We are one living,
breathing organism.

Did God breathe life into the dirt to create man, and then pull a rib from him to create woman? Or did God create a universe that allowed for the natural evolution of life? Maybe everyone is right. And yet, if He created it all, what difference does it make? If you're more comfortable believing the universe came from nothing and that everything is a random accident, that's okay, too. We do not have all the facts, and faith is not based in fact. That we are here at all is nothing short of astonishing — a wonderment — and there are too many missing pieces to that puzzle, perhaps all of them. There is really nothing to fight about.

Some three billion years ago, singled-celled organisms inhabited the Earth. In order to survive, they began to combine with one another, evolving into plants and animals. Finally, between 400,000 - 250,000 years ago, human beings began to appear. How did the cell know to combine with others unless it had some means of communication? We know the cell has a nervous system, digestive system, circulatory system, reproductive system, and even an immune system of sorts. Little mini beings, in so many ways like us. We like to think of ourselves as superior to these lesser forms of life. That's what our ego would like us to believe, so a god must have created us. Yet without these simpler forms of life we couldn't exist. We needed all those plants and animals in order to survive, and still do.

Each of the estimated 50 trillion cells it takes to make a human body has to know if it is a brain cell, lung cell, muscle cell, etc. And every cell holds 23 pairs of chromosomes containing our DNA (the blueprint for life). That would be 50 trillion times 23 pairs, equaling a staggering number of little blueprints, all knowing what they are to do. In order for the

DNA to direct the cells to the proper location in the body, it has to be swimming in the right nutrients. That's how they communicate. Gives new meaning to "We are what we eat!" Give a plant water and fertilizer and watch it grow; give it polluted water that confuses its signals, and watch it die. We are programmed to believe we inherit imperfections, but there is evidence that the right minerals and other essential nutrients can change those signals. Man cannot thrive on ice cream alone. We need those fruits, vegetables, nuts, grains, seeds, etc., in order for the communication to be clear.

Sometimes I wonder, when our body tells us that a big green salad sounds really good, or even if we just feel like crying, should we listen more closely to what it's telling us? It makes sense that there would be a guidance system for the health of our mental and physical body. So next time you have a craving or desire to laugh or to cry, pay attention. It could be just what your body needs. I'm not sure if I read this somewhere or if it's me, but it's stuck in my brain, so I'm passing it on to you. If we could keep laughter in a bottle and take it in pill form, there would be no depression. Laughter triggers the production and release of endorphins, and endorphins give a sense of well-being. The body is slow to recognize the pill we take to make endorphins, but it immediately recognizes laughter.

In the beginning, the Earth was toxic to any living organism. It was the impact of meteors with their life-giving deposit of minerals that changed our atmosphere. Miraculously, a perfect balance was achieved and life began. You could say we're made of stardust, but it was really the nutrients they brought with them. Was that by design or an accident?

Before the microscope, we didn't know about germs and bacteria. Absent knowledge of what causes disease and infection, we lived in fear of falling victim to them. Even God was fair game for blame, as many saw illness as punishment for their sins. We didn't understand the importance of cleanliness. Physical ills had nothing to do with sin and everything to do with the messages our body was not receiving due to the filth that had infiltrated and deranged it. With the advancements in science came antiseptics and antibiotics. However, in our ignorance we overused our antibiotic wonder drugs, enabling those little guys to adapt and become superbugs. Sadly, it was the use of antibiotics that showed overuse was not a good idea. Could we have anticipated and avoided this problem? Maybe, maybe not. I think we forget that the universe is perfectly designed, and that survival of living things is usually part of that design. I am relieved that dinosaurs didn't make it into this era. However their extinction may have been by design. Everything adapts and changes in order to survive.

Now we know that microorganisms are not inert, but very much alive and can communicate at some level, mutate, and evolve. Obviously, their drive to survive is every bit as strong as ours. Having that knowledge earlier would have perhaps prevented the superbug from evolving. So before we tinker with nature too much, for example by genetically modifying the crops that we grow, we need to pay attention to the lasting effects that our experimentation could have on us. Our bodies were designed to defend themselves, given proper nutrition, rest, and cleanliness. I'm not sure our bodies recognize genetically engineered food, preservatives, and additives. Also, let's not forget the toxins we spray our crops with and the chemicals we feed our animals. We know our digestive system has a harder time breaking down some of these foreign foods, but what else are they telling our cells to do or not do?

How do we feed the growing population without being able to produce bigger and hardier crops? How do you preserve them without additives? Factory-farmed livestock are given growth hormones and antibiotics to increase production, and we in turn consume them. It's a catch-22. It's possible we may have to go back to the basics one day. Hopefully, not at the expense of our children's health and development.

I love the (anonymous) little joke that Dr. Victor Bloom shares in *A Short History of Medicine*:

"Doctor, I have an earache."

2000 B.C. "Here, eat this root."

1000 B.C. "That root is heathen – say this prayer."

1850 A.D. "That prayer is superstition – drink this potion."

1940 A.D. "That potion is snake oil – swallow this pill."

1985 A.D. "That pill is ineffective – take this antibiotic."

2000 A.D. "That antibiotic is artificial – here, eat this root!"

Environmentalists and other informed humans are concerned that the perfect balance of Earth is being altered by the clear-cutting of oxygen-producing trees and the pollution of our water, air, and soil. Earth is the body our bodies live in. It's also clear that a clean and balanced environment – inside our bodies as well as outside – is essential for our cells to give and receive the right information. We are all one living breathing organism, so it is in our best interest to share and act upon these concerns.

There is only so much water on Earth; we can't make more water. Or at least, not yet. As we all know, it's two highly combustible elements combined (hydrogen and oxygen) that form this life-giving liquid. It's a mystery still. So, we have recycled the same water over and over since the beginning of time. When it's gone, it's gone. But have no fear! If we succeed in its destruction, the people will die but Mother Earth will begin to repair herself, allowing life to unfold again. I believe we will figure this out before it's too late. There is a growing awareness of the importance of global changes. They can't be ignored no matter how much money is to be made through the production of oil and coal, and the abuse of Earth's other resources. We are an intelligent species and I have faith we will discover what the balance in use and overuse is before it's too late. Perhaps we have figured it out and greed is slowing things down. In this case, I am forever hopeful of mans evolvement.

Beyond our grade-school science classes or what our religious leaders taught, most of us don't give much thought as to how we came to exist. Reading the *The Biology of Belief* by cellular biologist Bruce Lipton gave new meaning to me as to our interconnection to everything and insight into the miraculous little cell. Everything needs everything else to continue to evolve, as we've done since the Earth was formed and will continue to do so through centuries to come.

Wisdom from Chief Seattle: "Man did not weave the web of life – he is merely a strand in it. Whatever he does to the web, he does to himself." Evidently, the Chief knew then what science is finally discovering now.

Just to show how connected things are, let's look a little deeper into the cell. The cell is composed of molecules, and molecules are composed of atoms. It's safe to say that we and everything else are made of the same stuff, atoms. We are all the same. Everything solid is an illusion. I know I've made this point before, but it's worth repeating. We, and all you can see, are atoms held in place by energy fields. Can you imagine the fun science has with this? That's the world of quanta and where, I believe, all the answers are.

Next time you look at your friend, imagine that he or she is actually trillions of individual cells holding together to give the appearance of your very solid friend. So, "Beam me up, Scotty" from Star Trek doesn't seem so impossible. The transporter would scramble all the atoms and reassemble them in another location. No wonder Bones, the doctor, didn't like this means of transportation. After all, what if you were reassembled inside a tree or with an arm in the wrong place? Goof-ups notwithstanding, many discoveries have come from the fancies of science fiction. Maybe this will be one of them.

It seems impossible to me that the very first cell could have been an accident. Indeed, the wonder of a cell is unimaginable without a conscious intelligence behind it. How did that something begin without something to begin with? While many scientists of today would like to believe that something came from nothing, it was obvious to the cosmologists of ancient Greece that "nothing comes from nothing." Yet, some of our sharpest scientists hold that the possibility of a god is ridiculous. What do you think? Seems to me something came from something at some point. Was that something God?

Some believe as I do that God is pure consciousness, far beyond anything we can comprehend. "He" is certainly not a moody, anthropomorphic kind of creator, which is how many religions understand Him to be. "In the beginning was the Word, and the Word was with God, and the Word was God." (John 1:1) If the Bible were not so watered down by its many translators and editors, would we find some truths in it, given the knowledge we have today? I for one believe we would.

CHAPTER THIRTEEN

Fear and Love

Fear separates Earth from Heaven.
Every decision you make is accompanied
by one of these emotions.

Every feeling you have comes from the emotion of either fear or love. Negative emotion comes from fear, and happy emotion from love. Think about it for a moment and you'll see it's true. If you're mad or sad, ask yourself: *What about this situation am I afraid of?* Is it that you'll lose your power, possessions, your loved one, your health? Fear is paralyzing. What if this happens, or that? Most of the time it hasn't happened yet, and if it does, you can deal with it then. When you recognize the core fear it will put your problem into perspective and allow you to make conscious decisions. You can't stop life from happening; you can only move through it.

Bre belonged to me. I wanted to keep her with me forever and I still do. But she had her own agenda and purpose for being here. The illusion that she belonged to me was proven to be untrue. Appreciate the people and things you think belong to you and cherish every moment, because they indeed do not belong to you. They have their own purpose, and it's not the same as yours.

When my little girl was little, I saw myself as her protector. I lived in fear that she would hurt herself, or that something would happen to me and she would be alone. Fear begets fear. I wish I had devoted more time to her thoughts and feelings and less time to her physical state. I don't believe we leave before our time is up and our purpose is done. It would have been far more interesting knowing what she thought and how she felt about things than what her temperature was. I'm not suggesting that we let them walk into the fire, but there needs to be a balance, and that balance should be heavily weighted on the side of their thoughts, and not our fear of losing them. They won't leave before they're ready.

That's hard for me and many others to accept, but I now believe it is the truth.

As parents, we tend to blame ourselves when anything bad happens. *Why did I look away? Why wasn't I paying attention? I should have listened more closely! I was only gone for a second!* Blame creates deeper sadness and doesn't change anything. Try to move past the blame and into the deeper meaning. *Why are, or were, they here in the first place?* I feel so grateful for having known Bre and I wish I could have known her better. I thought I did, but when I talked to her friends, I realized there was so much more I could have known.

Imagine a world with no fear. Wouldn't that be heavenly? In fact, it does sound like the heaven that NDEers talk about. If the world we came from is all love, there would be no hard choices to make. The only choice to make in a loving environment would be how to become better, better and better. There would be no feelings of anger, jealousy, greed, revenge, etc. Just love. So how can He give us choices to make without creating a world of contrasts, such as fear and love? I spoke of the negative energy earlier. That is where fear – the devil, or Satan as some would call it-- lives. In order for us to experience life with choice, fear had to be introduced. Fear, not hate, is the opposite of love. Heaven is pure love, and Earth offers both. We now have a choice and a way to become better and better. He also, knew that we needed a way in and a way out— the human body is that way. The concept is simple; the complexity of making it happen is mind-boggling. Our bodies are temporary, not eternal.

There are numerous companies and nations that make money off your fears. Fear is a great motivator. Insurance companies remind you of your need of protection from financial ruin; many religions offer protection from hell (or a favorable place in the cosmos); vitamin companies are poised to protect your body by helping you to live longer, be healthier, lose weight, and gain muscle. War continues because we're afraid of people we don't understand, and intend to stop them before they stop us. Isn't that so? What or whom was wronged? Who gains the wealth or power from these fearful escapades? These are the issues we need to address before innocent people are caught up in yet another war, or we spend our money unnecessarily. Sadly, many of us don't or can't look much beyond what we are told, and so it goes, round and round.

It's unrealistic to think of a world without fear until we evolve beyond fear itself. I sometimes wonder if that is the true "plan". You can attempt to live without fear, which would be the first step. Being afraid doesn't change or improve anything – it just keeps you from thinking clearly and moving forward. Without fear, you would look at your actual needs and purchase only that insurance (or whatever thing) is truly needed. You might look more closely at all the supplements you take and choose only those that are definitely needed, or change your eating habits and save your money. People who feel oppressed or generally powerless are easily led to believe their problems are someone else's fault, and are so desperate they'll follow the leader who promises a better life. If war did stop, and nations began to build their infrastructures and feed their people with the money saved, war would become obsolete. Too bad most people can't yet embrace that simplicity, because it really could be that simple. Remove the fear and pay attention.

What if the fear of death were gone — completely gone — and we knew we were unconditionally loved and eternal beings? The brief moment we live on Earth would be just that, a brief moment — as poets would say, a "twinkling." We would still have some of the fears and anxieties of human beings, but they would have less urgency. Aging would be something to welcome and respect, as the natural flow of life. Death would be celebrated as a rebirth into another world or, as some say, "going home." No longer would it be regarded as the crushing conclusion that completely stops your world. The sadness you feel at losing someone would be buffered by the knowledge that you'll be together again.

I try to think of Bre as going on vacation to some exotic place she wanted to see. It is the longest vacation she has taken and a phone call would be wonderful. Sadly, the phone service is not good. She drops a note from time to time, although I wish there were more. I'll soon take that trip myself and join her in that purple and red tomato garden when my job is done.

We live in fear of not being loved and will do just about anything to "win" it. We put up walls, though, and withdraw within, for fear of being hurt when love is not felt. This fundamental insecurity increases over time, pushing love further and further away. Unconditional love can seem impossible to give or receive. Little children seem to have it. They have no walls up, but then again, they just left a world where that's all they knew. Our pets also have it. This is why most of us have a pet and why they are used for therapy in healing facilities. Imagine being bathed in love, completely accepted just as you are....What could be more gratifying, more healing?

Sadly, children soon learn that human love has conditions, or is nonexistent. It's safe to say love is by far the strongest emotion and, as I said earlier, the hardest to give or receive. Yet we all need it, and even crave it. Fear, on the other hand, comes easily. It's why most decisions are based in fear. If the decision feels good, I believe it is the right decision. Sometimes a decision can feel safe, but not particularly good. Is that just fear? What decision feels good, and not just safe? Maybe the decision is packed with fearful probabilities and you'll have to deal with the consequences of those probabilities, but your feeling is good about that decision. I try to lean toward the good feeling and deal with the consequences. Pay attention next time and see if the outcome over time is as it should be. I'm still waiting for an especially important decision I made to prove itself, but I'm confident it will and is. When a decision is based in love and the feeling is good, it is the right decision whether you personally see the outcome or not.

Egotism usually plays a role in making choices based in fear. We will "bite off our nose to spite our face" if it protects the ego. Too bad we can't put a gag on that little man in our head. He is always jabbering, and mostly it's negative. If you replace the "I" with "we," things will change in your life. By that I don't mean that others are more important than you. I mean we are equally important. Your views are yours and mine are mine. It's all okay. When we try to force our views on each other, it becomes all about feeding our egos. Nothing destroys relationships more than hungry egos. I hope you can see that.

"Fear is the root of all evil." We have all heard variations on that quote before. But, what is love? Love conquers not only fear but, in fact, "Love conquers all." The Bible says in Corinthians 13:4: *Love is patient, love is kind. It does not envy, it does not boast, it is not proud. It does not dishonor others, it is not self seeking, it is not easily angered, it keeps no record of wrongs. Love does not delight in evil but rejoices with the truth. It always protects, always trusts, always hopes, always perseveres.* That sounds true enough to me, but God's love is so much more! The unconditional love we speak so much about is completely accepting and all-consuming. We all wish someone would love us that way. Am I right? He does. But can we return His love as well? God gives it to everyone, every day. Why is it so hard for us to do the same? Fear, of course. After all, it might not be returned, but God is not afraid of that. God gave us a way around fear, but we don't always choose it because we're too afraid.

As my friend said after having an NDE, "It's a love I have never experienced here. That's how I know I wasn't here, and where I was, was real." It's complete acceptance with all your imperfections and no judgments, because in unconditional love there is no judgment or punishment – just an all-encompassing warmth. How would you feel if you felt loved like that? Would love ooze from you the way it would be oozing into you? It would, yes! You couldn't help it.

Our Creator gave us a way to live a beautiful life. Yet here we are, clinging to our ego with all its insecurities, at some level believing that if we let go, we'd lose ourselves. The opposite would be true. We would finally find ourselves.

Love is truly the most powerful, sought after energy on Earth and in the universe. Some say it is the only real energy.

CHAPTER FOURTEEN

In Conclusion

LOVE is all there is.

I didn't expect to find God when I started looking for Bre. In fact, I didn't know what to expect or what books I would start with. The facts are in science, yet science seemed beyond my grasp, and when you're in pain, the needed concentration is gone. When I was initially led to a book written by a medium, I was shocked. Yet I found hope in that and other similar books, and with hope came the desire to live. As I healed, the concentration necessary to dig deeper into more difficult works came. I developed an unquenchable thirst to solve the mystery of our true origin, which I hoped would lead me to Bre. But since no one, including those with much greater minds than my own, hadn't been able to prove anything, I didn't hold out much hope for my search. The NEED to find Bre drove me forward.

It was subtle at first, with a few "aha" moments. The first was when I realized that God is nothing like what I had been taught. He is so much greater! I began to see that He isn't like a human, but more like the energy that everything is made of. Now I believe He is bigger than that, far beyond our understanding. I no longer look up to find Him, but see Him all around me. The second realization was of the oneness and connection between all things, and the third was that every thought has an effect on the energy fields around us. I understood that God is not just in the universe; He is the consciousness of the universe – and beyond.

God doesn't see me or anyone this way, but I felt small and insignificant compared to the universe, yet for all my littleness, God saw my need to find Bre, and He wasn't afraid or censorious about where I looked. He doesn't care how you know

Him, as long as you know He cares and is with each and every one of us, His "little ones." Life is difficult, but He has your hand. The bad things will continue to happen here; He knows that. It was our choice to experience living with choice, and with that came the difficulties of life. The negativity, which accompanies fear, was the only way to realize a life of choice. Like a good father, He gave us what we wanted, but He didn't leave us alone. He loves us and always will. Many people tend to blame God when things go wrong, yet there is no one to blame. It is the wisdom gained by the experience that gives life purpose, and is why we chose – and choose – to live it.

The Bible teaches about choice and that it is ours to choose God through whatever religion or spiritual outlook we put our faith in. I put my faith in science because after all, He is the ultimate scientist. We tend to squeeze Him into little religious boxes when He is too large to fit into any one framework. Do you think He chooses to occupy any one box when He can be in all of them? The message to choose Him is correct, but not in any one particular way. It is to know Him and His love for you. He did not create this magnificence for all of us and then abandon us because of the particular specs of the box we put Him in. That would be our choice, not His.

I began to see the lines cross between science and the Bible and other holy books. I believe the early prophets were likely to have been men, trusting that their visions came from God. But regardless of their origin, divine or otherwise, the messages they received were filtered through their own belief systems. There may still be some truth in their words, especially if you can filter out or see through the assumptions of that day. When you don't have the knowledge of science, as they didn't when the scriptures were being written, you will try to make sense out of divine inspirations with the knowledge that you do have. That knowledge was based on myths and legends. They saw God as the big man in the sky, with the power to destroy or reward you. They got the "big" part right, but could not begin to fathom the immensity or the love. They had no knowledge of the universe or the energy in it. They "missed the mark," which is the definition of sin. Jesus came to put us back on track, but it seems we may still be missing the mark.

I wasn't looking for the one right religion to explain life to me. I didn't even know I was looking for God. I only wanted to know where and whether Bre still existed. And what I found was both a loving creator and a place we can all call home. The more I read and reflected on my reading, the clearer things became. He is the answer to all the mysteries we experience here. In retrospect, I wish I had been taking notes at the beginning of my search. I was only trying to survive. Three years into it, I knew I wanted to share my beliefs with Owen, and it was then that I began to write it all down. I can't be sure that reading my book will give him a true sense of God, but it is my hope that it will give him a reason to think of God in another way. God is and always will be his constant companion.

References

This is a list of books I have read over the years. I am sorry if there are some I have forgotten. I wasn't planning to write a book when I started, I was only trying to survive. They are the beliefs of the authors and not necessarily mine. I hoped to gather information that would prove to me, life is eternal and I would see Breana again. Faith simply wasn't enough.

The things you read, hear, see, and experience throughout your life form your beliefs. One thing I have learned in my life is nothing is certain, not even your beliefs. They are always subject to change. New discoveries in science happen everyday with new insights into a world that is unknown. There will never be THE END to discovery.

James Redfield—"Celestine Prophecy" the connection between all things in story form

Gregg Braden—"The God Code" is God coded into our DNA

Hazel Courteney—"Divine Intervention" a near-death experience leaving her with paranormal abilities

Sonya Choquette—"Diary of a Psychic"

Jan Frazier—"When Fear Fall Away" the release of fear, letting go and letting God

Gary Swartz Ph.D.—"The G.O.D. Experiments" proving God through science

Damien Broderick—"Outside the Gates of Science" is there a connection between quantum theory and paranormal

Dr. Jane Greer—"The Afterlife Connection" communicating with departed loved ones

Brian L. Weiss M.D.—"Many Lives Many Masters" a psychiatrists experiences with past life patients through hypnosis

Betty J. Eadie—"Embraced by the Light" a near-death experience

Robert Brown—"We Are Eternal" medium

Allan L. Botkin Psy.D.—"After Death Communication" a psychologist experience with visitations during patient therapy

Concetta Bertoldi—"Do Dead People Watch You Shower" medium

Sylvia Browne—"Mother God" the feminine side to God

Eckhart Tolle—"A New Earth" our attachment to ego and how to break free

Lee Carroll—"Indigo Children" are these children the beginning of the next human evolution

Sylvia Browne—"The Mystical Life of Jesus" a conspiracy theory, did Jesus die on the cross

Micheal Newton Ph.D.—"Destiny of Souls" life between life using hypnosis

Sylvia Browne—"Book of Angels" the description of angels through her guide

Lynn McTaggart—"The Field" scientific study of our interconnection through Zero Point Field [the energy around each cell]

Sylvia Browne—"Astrology Through a Psychics Eyes"

Sylvia Browne—"Book of Dreams"

Bill & Judy Guggenheim—"Hello From Heaven" after-death communication and experiences

Mary T Browne—"Life After Death" psychic view of where we go when we die

Char Margolis—"Questions From Earth, Answers From Heaven" psychic intuitive talks of life, death and beyond

Judith Orliff M.D.—"Second Sight" psychiatrist and intuitive speaks of discovering your own intuitive gift

Blair Underwood—"Before I Got Here" interviews with children

Sylvia Browne—"Contacting Your Spirit Guide" everyone has a guide and how to hear them

Squire Rushnell—"When God Winks" an executive with ABC who led Good Morning America to number one and his view of coincidence or synchronicity

Edited by Kent Nerburn—"The Wisdom of the Native American" Native American insights

Kenneth Ring Ph. D.—"Lessons From the Light" near-death experiences

Jim B. Tucker M.D.—"Life Before Life" children's memories of previous lives

Sylvia Browne—"Secret Societies"

Leslie M. Lecron—"Self Hypnosis"

Sanaya Roman & Duane Packer Ph.D.—"Opening To Channel" connecting with your guide

Chris Dufrestte—"My Life With Sylvia Browne her son's story

Gary Zukav—"The Seat of the Soul" becoming connected to your spirit who guides you, learning to pray and reincarnation

Barbara Marx Hubbard—"Conscious Evolution" the evolutionary path we are on

Carolyn Myss—"Entering The Castle" a journey into your soul, your true story

Dianne Arcangel—"Afterlife Encounters" study of a hospice worker on visitations

Don Piper—"90 Minutes in Heaven" his near-death experience

Sylvia Browne—"Conversations With the Other Side"

Carolyn Myss—"Sacred Contracts" discovering your purpose and divine potential

Dan Millman—"The Life You Were Born to Live"

Joseph Cambell—"Power of the Myth" study of myths and how they tie into religion

Sylvia Browne—"Secrets and Mysteries of the World"

Gordon Smith—"The Unbelievable Truth" medium

Sylvia Browne—"The Nature of Good and Evil"

Sylvia Browne—"Souls Perfection"

Sylvia Browne—"God Creation and Tools For Life"

Sylvia Browne—"Insight"

Sylvia Browne—"Phenomenon"

Sylvia Browne—"If You Could See What I See"

Sylvia Browne—"The Other Side and Back" The book I was led to read. There were two markers in this book, one in children and the other in death. Coincidence?

John Edwards—"After Life" medium

Bruce Lipton Ph.D.—"The Biology of Belief" cellular biologist explains how cells communicate and how our thoughts control life

Allison DuBois—"We Are Their Heaven" why the dead never leave us

Sylvia Browne—"Psychic Children"

John Edwards—"Crossing Over" medium

Neale Donald Walsch—"Conversations With God" he wrote a series of these books, they are his dialogues with God

OSHO—"The Book of Understanding" doubt and question everything you've been taught to believe

Gary E. Swartz Ph.D.—"The Afterlife Experiments" the research of an agnostic into the proof of God and his amazing experience

P.M.H. AtwaterL.H.D.—"Beyond the Indigo Children" the new generation of children being born

Joel Martin & Patricia Romanowski—"We Don't Die" interviews with George Anderson, a psychic medium

Gordon Smith—"Spirit Messenger" a barber/hairdresser by profession, tells of his experience as a medium

Allison DuBois— "Don't Kiss Them Goodbye" her story as a medium, she is also the person who inspired the NBC series "Medium"

Janis Amatuzio M.D.—"Beyond Knowing" a forensic pathologist on the conversations she had with family members of the deceased

Sylvia Browne—"Lesson for Life"

Squire Rushnell—"When God Winks at You" there are no coincidences

Rhonda Byrne—"The Secret" the universe brings what you believe you already have

Sylvia Browne—"Blessings from the Other Side"

Sylvia Browne—"Father God" masculine side of God

Meg Blackburne Lasey—"Children of the Now" are they misunderstood children of the future

Sylvia Browne—"Adventures of a Psychic"

Sylvia Browne—"Prophecy"

Colette Baron-Reid—"Remember the Future" discovering and developing you own intuitive gift

Sylvia Browne—"Visits from the Afterlife"

Lee Strobel—"The Case for Christ a detective gathers evidence for Christ

James Van Praagh—"Heaven and Earth" medium

Echo Bodine—"The Gift" learn to recognize your psychic gift

Sinclair Browning—"Feathers Brush My Heart" stories of mothers connecting to their daughters after death

Jerry Sittser—"A Grace Disguised" his personal struggle to find light in all the darkness after losing his mother, daughter and wife in auto accident

Kathy Cordova—"Let Go Let Miracles Happen: The Art of Spiritual Surrender" a three step process to experience the peace of surrender in any situation-learn to swim with the current of life

Arron Mitchell—"Death of an Ordinary Life" a mystery novel of a spiritual journey to forgiveness-Aaron is a gifted psychologist and also my nephew

Marianne Williamson—"The Age of Miracles" a spiritual look at aging gracefully

Kim Sheridan—"Animals and the Afterlife" if you love and respect animals, as I do, this is an uplifting book to read

Neale Walsch—"Happier Than God"

Elizabeth Gilbert—"Eat Pray Love" finding herself and God

Sylvia Browne—"End of Days" future predictions

Micheal Books—"13 Things That Don't Make Sense" scientific mysteries

Alberto Villodo Ph.D.—"Mending the Past and Healing the Future With Soul Retrieval" a medical anthropologist who came to be a shaman and why

Bryon Katie—"Loving What Is" living without fear and the four questions to ask yourself

Bill Bryson—"A Short History of Nearly Everything"

Dan Millman—"The Laws of the Spirit" bullet point laws of spirit

Dan Millman—"Wisdom of the Peaceful Warrior" companion to "Way of the Peaceful Warrior" spiritual insights into living a peaceful life in story form

Rosemary Brown—"Immortal by My Side" medium

Francis S Collins—"The Language of God: A scientist Presents Evidence for Belief" bridging the gap between science and God

Max Lacado—"Fearless" Christian view of sin

Tara Singh—"Nothing Real Can Be Threatened" a philosophy

Bruce Lipton Ph.D. and Steve Bhaerman—"Spontaneous Evolution" our positive future based in science and with his usual humor

Deepak Chopra—"How to Know God"

Colin Wilson—"Afterlife" a journalist documents evidence of another life after death

Paulo Coelho—"The Alchemist" a novel of the treasure within

Betty Eadie—"Embraced by the Light" an afterlife experience

Sylvia Browne—"Accepting the Psychic Torch"

Brian Greene—"The Elegant Universe" how the universe and life began from what science knows today

Trudy Harris RN—"Glimpses of Heaven: True Stories of Hope and Peace at the End of Life's Journey"

Joan Wester Anderson—"Guardian Angels: True Stories of Answered Prayer"

Todd Burpo & family—"Heaven is for Real: A Little Boy's Astounding Story of His Trip to Heaven" near-death experience

Mary Evelyn Tucker—"Journey of the Universe" how we fit into the 14 billion year history of the universe, weaving science and wisdom of the ages

James Van Praagh—"Looking Beyond" medium

James Van Praagh—"Unfinished Business" medium

Joan Wester Anderson—"Where Miracles Happen" stories of modern day miracles and how God still makes himself known to us today

Micheal Singer—"The Untethered Soul" the voice in your head who continually talks to you should be given a name and a hat to wear

Julia Assante PhD,M.D. and Larry Dossey—"The Last Frontier: Exploring the Afterlife and Transforming Our Fear of Death" an anthropologist presents evidence of life after death

Eben Alexander III M.D.—"Proof of Heaven" an unbelieving neurosurgeon has a near-death experience changing him forever

Maggie Callanan and Pat Kelley—"Final Gifts" experiences of hospice nurses

Joel S. Goldsmith—"The Thunder of Silence" being one with God-the hidden meaning of "sermon on the mount"

Elsa Barker—"Letters from the Afterlife" medium

Esther and Jerry Hicks—"The Vortex" the law of attraction

Esther and Jerry Hicks—"The Astonishing Power of Emotion" the role emotion plays in the laws of attraction

Esther and Jerry Hicks—"Ask and It is Given"

Fred A. Wolf—"Taking the Quantum Leap: The New Physics for Nonscientists" traces the history of physics and our relationship to the cosmos

Fred A. Wolf—"Dr. Quantum's Little Book of Big Ideas" where science meets spirit

Nick Herbert—"Quantum Reality: Beyond the New Physics" an introduction to physics-the scientific and philosophical controversy

Sandra Anne Taylor—"Quantum Success: The Astounding Science of Wealth" a formula for success and an abundant life

Tara Singh—"Nothing Real Can Be Threatened: Exploring a Course in Miracles" a philosophy

Larry Dossey M.D.—"Recovering the Soul" how to pray etc."thy will be done"- quantum physics-non local and local realities

Steve Volk—"Fring-ology: How I Tried to Explain Away the Unexplainable-And Couldn't" a journalist's journey into the unknown

Anthony Borgia—"Life in the World Unseen" medium who claims to channel Monsignor Robert Hugh Benson speaking from the afterlife

Fred Alan Wolf—"Mind Into Matter: A New Alchemy of Science and Spirit" thought provoking look at consciousness

Susan Blackmore—"Dying to Live" a near death experience

Ernest Holmes—"The Hidden Power of the Bible" a deeper look at scripture through a scientific mind

Gregg Braden—"The Divine Matrix" an aerospace computer systems designer and computer geologist tells of our connection and role we have in the quantum stuff that rules us.

Brian Weiss M.D.—"Only Love is Real" past life regression

Louise Hay—"You Can Heal Your Life" the mental patterns that create physical illness

Lynn McTaggart—"The Intention Experiment" the effect your thoughts have on things

Neale Walsch—"Home With God" a conversation with God

Tom Brown jr.—"The Quest" a mans search for peace and insight

Dan Millman—"The Journey of Socrates" a novel in spiritual advice

John Edwards—"After Life" medium

Jeff Guidry—"An Eagle Named Freedom" a beautiful story of love and healing

Dan Millman—"Sacred Journey of the Peaceful Warrior" spiritual novel of peace and understanding

Wm. Paul Young—"The Shack" a welcome look at God and eternity written in story form

John Lerma M.D.—"Into the Light" stories of extraordinary experiences by a hospice doctor

Joseph McMoneagle—"Memoirs of a Psychic Spy" the life of a remote viewer and his work with the U.S. government

Caroline Myss Ph.D.—"The Creation of Health" the effect emotion has on health

Randy Alcorn—"Heaven" a Biblical evaluation of Heaven with the use of scripture

Alan Cohen—"Handle With Prayer" how to pray

Alan Cohen—"Wisdom of the Heart" insights

Doug Ell—"Counting to God"

TobinHart Ph.D.—"The Secret Spiritual World of Children"

Gerald G. Jampolsky, MD—"Love is Letting Go of Fear"

Pam Grout—"E Squared" experiments proving power of thought

Patricia Pears—"Opening Heaven's Door" stories of life, death and what comes after

Theresa Caputo—"There's More to Life Than This" medium

Emanuel Swedenborg—"A Swedenborg Sampler" theologian and philosopher 1688-1772

Gerald G. Jampolsky, MD—"Love Is Letting Go Of Fear"

Hope R. Reynolds—"What Is Heaven"

April Crawford—"In The Afterlife"

Pamela Heath and Jon Klimo—"Handbook to the Afterlife"

Dennis and Nolene Prince—-"Nine Days In Heaven" a rewrite of the original book *Scenes Beyond The Grave*

Diana Stuart—"Journey To The Other Side" a near-death experience

Rod Pennington and Jeffery A. Martin—"The Fourth Awakening" mystery novel with an interesting analogy of man's evolution in Chapter 15

AND I AM STILL READING

Query

When faith is not enough, where do you turn? The things we learn as children become the facts we base many decisions on. Are they true—or just accepted and passed down through time? *When You Think About It* is my personal journey into some of these truths.

In 2006 I lost my only child and life line. I had to have answers. Faith was not enough. Where were the facts? I read books by mediums, doctors, and scientists. I began to see lines cross between science and religion. It made me want to know more. What do quantum physics, near-death experiences, biology, and reincarnation have in common? Or is there a commonality? I read several books in each category in order to write one book connecting all categories. It was interesting that I hadn't found a book with all subjects covered in one. Had no one else seen the connection? This research led me to a truly loving God, the ultimate scientist, and the thought behind all that is.

I wrote the book to inform my grandson, who never knew his mother, of the eternal being he is, and that he'll meet his mom one day. It became evident that others wanted to read it, too.

My name is Cynthia Mitchell. I have been a hairdresser since 1971 and have owned a successful salon since 1986. During that time I have had the opportunity to speak and teach at hair seminars with large groups of people. It has been my pleasure to educate and encourage new hair designers. Over the years I have been a counselor, mediator, and friend to many. Life is my teacher, as it is for all of us.

CPSIA information can be obtained at www.ICGtesting.com
Printed in the USA
BVOW08*1324140415

395730BV00004B/8/P